編者的話

　　台灣邁向國際化、自由化的腳步日漸加快，相對地也增加了國人活躍在國際舞台的機會。因此現代企業人除了要具備尖端專業技術之外，還必須培養辯才無礙的**口才**與靈活的**交際手腕**，才能在國際商業往來中，主動出擊，完成任務。

　　但對國人而言，用國語面對一大群人做演說，都還會怯場，更何況是用英語。**缺乏練習**及**經驗不足**是主要原因，有鑑於此，我們特別編成這本「**商務英語演說**」（**Business Speech & Communication**），提供現代企業人，用英語致詞及發表演說的原則與技巧。

　　本書將現代商業活動中，各式場合的演說、致詞加以整理，分為以下三類：

(1) **Ceremonial Speech**：包括迎新（**Greeting Newcomers**）、送舊（**Bidding Farewell**）、喜宴（**Wedding Reception**）、開幕（**Opening a New Branch**）、接受頒獎（**Receiving An Award**）等各式**社交聯誼場合致詞**。篇篇輕薄短小，凝聚全場焦點。

(2) **Informative Speech**：囊括企業及公司部門簡介、產銷程序報告、市調報告（**Market Research**）、推銷產品（**Sale's Talk**）等多篇**業務會報**，讓外國客戶對您刮目相看。

(3) **Persuasive Speech**：模擬國際場合中，被要求即席針對國內受人爭議的主題做說明。舉凡國內投資環境（**Investment Environment**）、環保政策（**Environmental Protection**）、仿冒問題（**Piracy**）、保護主義（**Protectionism**）等皆包括在內。教您舉一反三，贏得國際友誼，從表現自我中，肯定自我。

●CONTENTS●

業務簡報演說
CHAPTER 3　Informative Speeches
107

CHAPTER 4 即席專題演說
Persuasive Speeches

165

Chapter

1

認識商務英語
演說

Business
Speeches

1
Unit

商業英語演說的基礎理論
The Basic Theories of Business Speeches

在眾人面前演說（Public Speech），是指單獨一個人，針對某個主題（Topic），以多數聽眾爲對象所進行的溝通行爲。美國人非常重視*"Public Speaking"*，各高中、大學都視爲 **必修科目**。在美國社會中，有能力的*Public Speaker* 也比較容易獲致成功的機會，其重要性可想而知。近年來，邁向商業國際化的我國，也逐漸有這種傾向。

如果把 Public Speaking 當做是一種溝通的行爲，我們就必須先了解「何謂溝通？」。有些學者認爲：「溝通是積極或眞心誠意地和對方說話」，但這個定義還不夠明確。

本章中將介紹有關溝通（ *Communication* ）的三個理論，以俾讀者能進一步瞭解溝通的過程與內容。

第一理論：溝通七要素

第一個溝通理論，以語言為媒介，是人類最普遍的溝通行為。美國威斯康辛大學史蒂芬‧魯卡斯教授指出，任何種類的溝通，都由以下七個要素所構成：

① **說話者**（ *Speaker* ）
② **訊息**（ *Message* ）
③ **媒介**（ *Channel* ）
④ **傾聽者**（ *Listener* ）
⑤ **回饋**（ *Feedback* ）
⑥ **妨礙‧干涉**（ *Interference* ）
⑦ **狀況**（ *Situation* ）

關於①「**說話者**」和④「**傾聽者**」，並不需要多做說明。因為如果沒有說話者和傾聽者，溝通就無法成立。

②「**訊息**」指的是在溝通行為中，所要傳遞的內容和消息。換言之，就是「自己想要說的話以及想要讓人知道的事」。這句話乍看之下，也許會令讀者以為傳遞訊息並不難。但事實上，要人不誤解「自己想表達的意思（ *Intended Message* ）」，比想像中還要困難。尤其是用英語來溝通，往往很難將這個 Intended Message 表達得很清楚。

例如和外國公司做生意時，由於談不攏必須放棄這項交易，但又不想和該公司完全斷絕生意關係。碰到這種情況時，雖然委婉地說：" *Give us some time to consider this matter.* "（請給我們一點時間考慮看看。），對方也不見得會瞭解說話者的 Intended Message（即，這筆生意就談到這裡吧！），而往往產生完全相反的反應（例如，「要等多久才會有結論？」）。

③「**媒介**」指的是傳遞的方法。如：語言、肢體語言（**Body Language**）、電話、電視、無線電等。

⑤「**回饋**」指的是溝通進行中對方的反應。這可從對方的語言及肢體語言上來發覺。譬如，傾聽者附和著說：「嗯！」，這就是他在仔細聽說話者談話的「回饋」。至於皺眉頭、打哈欠也是一種「回饋」，但這是表示傾聽者對說話者的談話，感到**厭煩、沒興趣**的意思。

⑥「**妨礙・干涉**」又稱為「噪音」。比方說，當你在演講時，會場外傳來陣陣尖銳的電鑽聲，使得你和聽衆無法心平氣和地進行溝通，這就是溝通行為中的「妨礙・干涉」。

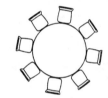

⑦「**狀況**」指的是溝通上的 TPO（Time, Place, Occasion）——**時間，地點，場合**。例如，在結婚典禮上提到離婚的事並不恰當；敬酒時講了長篇累綴的話，也令人覺得無趣。所以，不論什麼形式的溝通，都會受到當時狀況的影響。因此，必須懂得看場合做演講。

以上所說只是一般性的溝通而已，接下來要介紹與商業活動結合的溝通理論。

第二理論：戴爾卡耐基

戴爾・卡耐基（*Dale Carnegie*）出生於美國密蘇里州的農家，州立師範大學畢業後，擔任過教師、職員、演員、推銷員等工作，其後創立了「**卡耐基教室**」，幫助人們發展演說的潛在特質，目前已擁有了一百萬名的畢業生。他根據自己豐富的工作經驗，寫了好幾本深具效果的商業溝通秘訣（know-how），如：" *How to Develop Self-Confidence and Influence People by Public Speaking* "（「如何建立自信及用演說影響他人」）、" *Public Speaking and Influencing Men in Business* "（「商用演說術與影響」）、" *How to Win Friends and Influence People* "（「如何贏得友誼和影響力」）等。這些著作都成為暢銷書，不只是商人，就連一般大眾在人際關係及演講方面，都受到他很大的啟發。其中「如何贏得友誼和影響力」，同時是「卡內基教室」和 YMCA 演講課程的課本。在過去二十年中，它被翻譯成二十多種不同的語言，銷售了數千萬本。

　　上述三本書有個共同點，就是書名上都有" Influence "這個字。也就是說，在卡耐基的想法中，溝通的目的是在「影響對方」。在此把這種以 Influence 為目的的溝通方式，稱為" **Influence-based Communication** "（以影響力為主的溝通）。其基本構想可用下面這個簡單的圖形來表示：

　　Source 是「消息來源」，相當於第一溝通理論中的「說話者」（Speaker）；Target 是「目標」，相當於「傾聽者」（Listener）。卡耐基分別用 Source 和 Target 來代替 Speaker 和 Listener，用意在

把溝通的對象，當做獵人狙殺的獵物（目標），以演講為手段來改變對方的價值觀、態度和信念。這正是卡耐基溝通理論的主要宗旨。

這種「以影響力為主」的溝通理論，在競爭激烈的商場，更能發揮效果。例如，在和客戶交涉或推銷新產品時，只要先設定一個*Target*（目標），然後想辦法去影響那個Target（目標），讓對方產生與我們做生意的興趣，進而購買公司的產品。所以，企業家應該傾全力創造影響目標（Target）的訊息（Message）。與其把客戶、消費者當做「人」或「聽衆」，不如把他們視爲目標（Target），以各式各樣的message 來加以攻擊。這就是美國商場上常見的“*Hard Sell*”（硬性推銷）！

美國的推銷員不管在什麼情況之下，都必須像連珠炮一樣，把許多資訊喋喋不休地說出來，以期能在極短的時間內，使對方陷入**資訊超載**（*Information Overload*）之中，而喪失理性的判斷力，這也是一種商場作戰方式。

此外，美國的電視廣告大多是根據*hard sell* 的原則來製作的。類似以下這種攻擊性（ aggressive）的廣告佔了一大半：例如用實驗的方式和其他公司同類產品做比較，來突顯自己產品的優點；要不然就是列出自己產品的優點及長處，向觀衆積極地推銷。

以硬性推銷（*Hard Sell*）爲基礎的溝通，是各國商界人士普遍接受的觀念。直到現在，仍深根蒂固地被當做商業活動的基本理念。但是，這個溝通理論一走上極端，可能會過份強調影響力（*Influence*），而以操縱（*Manipulate*）做爲主要目的，最後則像操作機器一樣，毫無忌憚地操縱目標（Target）的意志和想法。換句話說，這個溝通理論具有漠視對方感受與忽略人際關係的缺點，因此不見得會產生自己預期的效果。

第三理論：人際關係

有些學者針對「**以影響力爲主的溝通**」（*Influence-based Communication*）的缺點，提出了把重點置於**人際關係**上的商業溝通理論。1960 年代，以演講爲著眼點的美式人際關係學課程中，開始出現「人際溝通」（Interpersonal Communication）這類的講座，強調「*相互瞭解*」（*Mutual Understanding*）比「*影響力*」（*Influence*）重要。商業溝通理論無可避免地也受到極大的影響。

主張以人際關係爲中心的雙向商業溝通理論的人士，年年在增加，南伊利諾大學的詹姆斯・凡奧斯丁（James VanOosting）教授也是其中的一位。根據他的理論，溝通可用下面的圖形來表示：

Message 指的是「**訊息、內容、措詞**」，*Relationship* 指的是「**人際關係**」（即第 1 理論中魯卡斯教授所說的 *Situation*），廣義有前後關係、狀況（Context）的意思。凡奧斯丁教授認爲：「**在以商業溝通爲**

主的任何溝通中，必定存在著某些「人際關係」（ *Relationship* ），並且在這個架構上，進行各種訊息（ *Message* ）的交換」。

例如，父子間的對話，與同事、上司或部屬交談，以及推銷員向顧客推銷，都是基於某種人際關係的溝通。

	Influence-based Communication	Relationship-based Communication
1. 目　　的	Influence and Control	Understanding（理解）
2. 溝通過程	One-Way（Unilateral）	Two-Way（Bilateral）
3. 商業溝通	Persuade & Hard Sell	Maintain Relationships & Soft Sell

總之，第 2 溝通理論的目的，在影響對方的想法或行為，並且控制對方的行動以配合自己的目的，因此多採取「**單向溝通**」（ *one-way* ），不理會人際關係，只重視如何創出有利於己的訊息（ message ）。而第 3 溝通理論，則以相互瞭解為目的，重點在與對方交換意見與想法，因此屬「**雙向溝通**」（ *two-way* ），是一種聊天式而非以上壓下的說話方式，強調和睦的氣氛，以創出有助於彼此了解的訊息（ message ）為重點。

人類所有溝通行為，大致上可分為上述兩種類型，而商業演說或商業溝通也不外乎這兩種方式。英語商業演說，根據其目的有時需要第 2 溝通的演說，有時也需要第 3 溝通的演說。關於這一點，**Unit 2 英語演說的種類**中，再詳加說明。

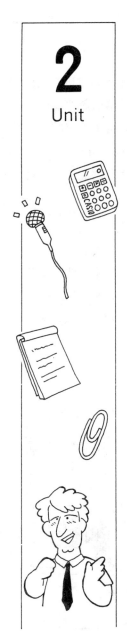

2

Unit

商業英語演說的種類

Three Types of Business Speeches

　　商業社交演說按照狀況、人際關係與目的，大致上可分爲以下三種：

① **Ceremonial Speech** （典禮上的演說）

② **Informative Speech** （傳遞訊息的演說）

③ **Persuasive Speech** （說服性的演說）

典禮上的演說

　　第一種*Ceremonial Speech*，指的是各種聯誼場合及慶弔儀式上的演說。主要是表示歡迎、祝賀、哀悼、激勵等之意。其最大的目的，是透過這類的活動，使人際關係更爲密切、熟絡。

　　可見這類演說是以**人際關係**爲中心的溝通行爲，屬第三理論的溝通方式，因此較注重演講時的**氣氛**和**表達方式**。

傳遞訊息的演說

第二種 *Informative Speech*，是指傳遞對方所不知道的訊息及知識的演說，內容包括**發表新產品、介紹公司企業**和**發佈人事調動**等。關於這方面的演說，如果只是單調地傳達訊息，必然令人覺得索然無味。所以需要在編排上花一些工夫。這類的演說是以訊息（ message ）為中心，但與聽眾的關係也很密切，是介於第二理論和第三理論之間的溝通行為。

說服性的演說

最後Persuasive Speech，是演說者與他人的意見發生分歧時，想將他的主張或想法傳給聽眾，以尋求解決之道的演說。此類型演說的目的在**改變**對方的想法或態度，進而和自己的意見**趨於**一致。所以是屬於典型的第二理論的溝通。

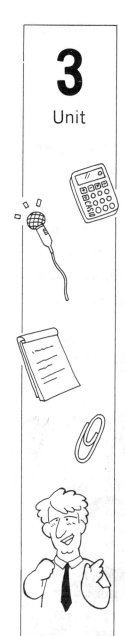

3
Unit

如何克服講台恐懼症
How to Overcome Stage Fright

　　即使是演講次數再頻繁的人，在開講的前一刻鐘，也會因**自我焦慮**而感到緊張，何況是從小就缺乏演說訓練的國人，第一次面對觀衆時會有「**講台恐懼症**」了。但這種恐懼症是每位演說者必經的過程，**馬克‧吐溫**（ *Mark Twain* ）第一次上講台時，口中有如塞著一團棉布，而且心跳加速，好像剛跑完百米賽跑一樣，**林肯總統**也曾在衆目睽睽之下，因害羞而說不出話來。

　　但要如何才能跨越這層障礙，輕鬆自如地在衆人面前演說呢？以下四項建議可以幫助你在上台前，做好心理建設：

以強烈的企圖心爲起始

　　想想這次演說將爲你帶來朋友、客戶、個人影響力及增强你的統御能力；也就是列舉出演說能力會帶給自己的**好處**，引發你對它的狂熱及企圖心；並告訴自己要以壯士斷腕，破斧沈舟的決心，做一場完美的演出。

知道所要談的內容

在面對觀眾的時候，除非你已想好了談話的主題與內容，否則是不可能感到舒適的。以下就演說種類的不同，分項介紹準備的原則。

① *Ceremonial Speech*：一般社交聯誼場合上的致詞，最怕的就是即席式地邀請出席者上台說幾句應景的話。而台上的聽眾也不要求你說出一篇大道理，只要說些與這次聚會相關的事即可。因此；平常你就應該分析自己常參加的社交場合，事先擬好各種場合的應景演說，想像自己隨時會被請上台去，以免到時慌了手腳。

② *Informative Speech*：以簡報性質為主的演說，多半是事前就知道主題，因此所謂的準備，就是指收集足夠的**資料**，草擬一份演講稿。

③ *Persuasive Speech* ：此類演說以說服他人為目的，因此，**舉證資料的收集**，是最重要的準備工作。平時可將各類報紙、雜誌上的重要新聞，統計資料，甚至笑話、軼聞剪下來，分門別類的收集起來，將來絕對用得上。唯有見聞廣博的人；才會是個優秀的演說家。此外，這種準備工作也有助於即席演說時，讓你在三秒鐘之內決定所要談的內容與主題。

假裝信心十足的上台

「**最好的防衛就是進攻**。」，因此你必須先練習假裝無懼地上台，只要你能持久，漸漸地就能弄假成眞了。

當你站在台上時，特別在說服性的演說中，先將身體挺直，正視聽衆，想像他們都欠你一大筆錢，義正辭嚴地開始。千萬不要將上衣釦子開了又扣，扣了又開，頻頻拭汗或玩弄手指等，這樣只會讓你更緊張而已。如果你一定要做些動作來緩和情緒，可將手背在後面用力扭曲，擺動腳趾或在手掌握住一枚硬幣，至少別讓台下看見。有時展示某件東西，在黑板上寫寫字，或在地圖上指出一個位置也會使你覺得更自在一些。

練習、練習、再練習

恐懼多半來自**未知**及**缺乏信心**，而不知道自己是否有能力可完成又是缺乏信心的成因；因此只要你有過順利完成的經驗，害怕自然會消失。一般人的天賦都是差不多的，唯有不斷的練習，才會使他越來越能應付。想辦法，在上台前替自己創造經驗吧！如果可能的話，先講給三、五個朋友聽看看。若是一人獨自練習，也要努力地**想像**面前坐著一群眞正的聽衆，以致於當你眞正面對聽衆時，你已擁有舊經驗了。當然別忘了用**錄音機**錄下你的演說，自己聽聽看。

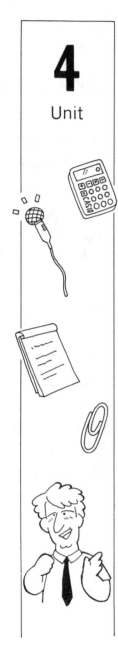

4
Unit

如何構思演說內容
How to Plan a Speech

英語演說有三個重要的架構：

① **Introduction** （開場白）
② **Body** （本論）
③ **Conclusion** （結論）

原則上**序論**（ *Introduction* ）和**結論**（ *Conclusion* ）的內容較短，**本論**（ *Body* ）則較長。以下分項說明。

開場白

開場白（ *Introduction* ）是演說中最重要的部分，也是給聽眾的第一印象，更是決定是否引起聽眾興趣的關鍵。

在開場白中必須明示演說的目的和主題。例如在典禮上的演說，開場白是以「**引起注意、製造氣氛**」

為目的。至於傳遞訊息和說服性的演說，則以「**使主題明確和引起聽眾興趣**」為目的。由此可見開場白的作用是「**提出問題**」。

本論

如果說開場白（ Introduction ）和結論（ Conclusion ）是演說的框架，那麼**本論**（ *Body* ）就是裝在裡面的東西。這是最吸引聽眾的部分，在談到如何有效地編寫本論之前，必須先認識下面三個字：

(1) *Outline* （大綱）

(2) *Main Points* （主要論點；主旨）

(3) *Supporting Data* （支持論點的資料；舉證）

首先談到的是**大綱**（ *Outline* ）。建築房子需要設計圖，旅行時必須有周密的行程表（ Itinerary ）。同樣的道理，好的演說也要有完備的大綱（ Outline ）。演講者必須先在大綱中把自己所主張的**主要論點**（ *Main Points* ）列出來，然後寫下支持主要論點的**資料**（ *Supporting Data* ），才能完成一篇本論（ Body ）的計劃表。

主要論點（ *Main Points* ）指的是演講者想要表達的想法或主張。在準備本論（ Body ）的階段中，最好能夠按照1,2,3…的步驟，將主要論點（ Main Points ）列出來。

以蓋房子為例，**主要論點**（ *Main Points* ）和挖地基、架樑柱一樣。如果不知道該使用什麼樣的柱子，也不瞭解一根根柱子必須打在哪裡，就無法建造出一棟美侖美奐的房子。

　　柱子打入地下後，還需要砌上牆磚和各種補強材料，這就是 ***Supporting Data***（支持論點的資料）。只有柱子還不能算蓋好了房子，必須有了牆壁才能顯出柱子的功用。

　　Supporting Data 按照字面上的意思來看，指的是能夠使 Main Points 更具有說服力的客觀事實。演講者平常就應該多搜集 Supporting Data。其範圍非常廣泛，可以取材自**統計資料、書籍、報章雜誌**和**專家的意見**等。

　　總之，在**大綱**（ *Outline* ）中必須寫下**主要論點**（ *Main Points* ）和**支持論點的資料**（ *Supporting Data* ），這是準備演講時不可欠缺的步驟。

　　以下是 Outline 的一個範例：

─< Outline >─

Ⅰ. **Regular jogging provides several everyday benefits :**
（ Main Point 1 ）

　　A. It increases your endurance. （Supporting data 1 ）
　　B. It improves your sleeping pattern. （data 2 ）
　　C. It helps control your weight. （data 3 ）

Ⅱ. **Jogging has become much more popular in the last decade.**（ Main Point 2 ）

　　A. Millions of people have taken up jogging.
　　　（Supporting data 1 ）
　　B. Sales of running shoes and sweat suits have risen dramatically. （data 2 ）
　　C. Newspapers now have regular columns about jogging.
　　　（data 3 ）

　　Main Points的**數目**，按演講時間的長短來決定，但最好訂在**三個或三個以下**，太多的話會使聽眾不容易消化。三個左右的Main Points可以**減少**聽眾的負擔，讓他們較能夠**瞭解**演說者的意向。

　　此外，如果演講的時間只有短短的幾分鐘，就**必須**集中火力於一個Main Point上，效果較佳。

結論

　　講稿最後的部分稱為**結論**（*Conclusion*），為了幫助聽眾瞭解及加深印象，將演說內容做個簡短的**歸納**，這就是結論（Conclusion）的功用。有時候Main Points也可以當做結論。但如果演講者以為自己想要說的話，必須保留到結論中才講就錯了。一般而言，英語演講都把**主張**或**結論**，放在Body的開頭來敍述，這和國人的習慣不太一樣。

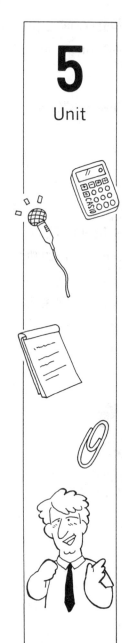

5
Unit

社交演說的禮儀與技巧
Perfecting Your Speech

在準備好講稿後，你可能會放心地說：「萬事OK！」。但現在是要用**英語**來演講，所以必須注意到與用國語演講時，各種不同的**禮儀**和**技巧**。

艾蜜莉・波斯特（*Emily Post*）女士可說是美國的禮儀專家，她生前常接受各報章雜誌的訪問，談了許多有關禮儀方面的問題，而且深入社會生活中的各個層面。她所寫的 " *Emily Post's Etiquette* "，被認爲是社會生活、社交和溝通行爲的聖經，受到美國一般大衆的喜愛和閱讀。

社交演說禮儀

她的孫女**伊莉莎白・波斯特**（*Elizabeth Post*）也出版了 " *The New Emily Post's Etiquette* " 這本書。書中談到了有關演說（ Public Speaking ）的禮儀和技巧。她特別提出下面五點：

① **問候語**（ *Opening Word* ），這是演講前的開場白。在正式的場合中，一站到講台上就應該面向主席，感謝他爲自己做介紹。如：" *Mr. Chairman, thank you very much for your kind introduction.* "

如果有上司等重要貴賓（ VIP ）在場時，也要在問候語中提到他。如：" *Mr. President, Distinguished guests, Ladies and Gentlemen* "。如果知道來賓的**姓名**，最好也能說出他們的姓名。

② **運用幽默及輔助道具**（ *Use Humor and Props* ）。其中"props"是 property 的略字，意謂「**小道具**」。波斯特女士指出，**笑話、逸聞、名言**也包括在「幽默」之中，這些可使談話內容更加生動、有趣。

至於「小道具」指的是視聽器材、幻燈片的銀幕、教鞭（ *pointer* ）等。在傳遞正確訊息的 Informative Speech 中，或是表明自我主張的 Persuasive Speech 中，有了這類的「小道具」更能發揮演講的威力。

③ **聲音恰到好處**（ *The Importance of Your Voice* ）。聲音的高低、大小、音質和說話的速度，與演講的內容同樣重要。

音質是天生的，無法更改，但**聲音的大小**和**朗讀的速度**却是可以改進的。如果會場很大、聽衆又多，而又沒有麥克風時，就必須拉高嗓門讓所有的聽衆聽得見。相反的，使用麥克風時，不要把嘴巴湊得太近，免得讓聽衆覺得震耳欲聾。所以，在演講之前，可以坦率地問聽衆: " *Can you hear me all right* ? " 或 " *Is my voice loud enough* ? "

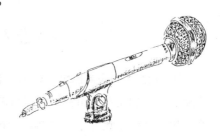

　　根據波斯特女士的說法，朗讀的速度一分鐘差不多是 **90～130 個字**。但我們不是以英語為母語，所以會比這個標準慢一點。此外，若老是用同樣的速度演講，就像唸經一樣，會令人覺得無趣，所以偶爾也要改變一下說話的速度。

　　④ **長話短說**（ *The Danger of Rambling* ）。" rambling "是「喋喋不休」的意思。任何演講都有時間上的限制，若無視於時間限制，而喋喋不休地大談特談，不但浪費時間、破壞氣氛，也會招致出席者或其他演說者的反感。

　　但讀者若能將 **Introduction**、**Body**、**Conclusion** 的構成方法謹記在心，大概就不致於 Rambling 了。

　　⑤ **漂亮結尾**（ *In Closing* ）。俗諺說："*All's well that ends well.*"（好的結束就是一切都美好。）。正如這句話所說，結束演講的方式也很重要，千萬不要說出"*That's all.*"，"*The end.*"這類草率的話。簡單地做個**歸納**，就是一種好的結束方式。另外，用**幽默**的語氣或**笑話**做總結，可以加深聽眾的印象。或者也可用向聽眾表示**謝意**來結束演講，如："*I want to thank you all for your attention.*"。但不論用哪一種方式，在演講前就應該決定好。

演說技巧

　　① **在演講中表達感情**：任何一篇演講都包括事實的敘述和演講者的意見。兩者相比較，可知道闡述自己意見的部分比敘述事實的部分，更容易加入感情。此外，在段落改變的地方，感情也隨之而產生變化。而疑問句、會話的部分也比其他部分更能表露感情。

但要如何表達自己的情感呢？以下四點可供讀者參考：

- a. **調整聲音的高低**
- b. **加上手勢動作**
- c. **改變說話速度**
- d. **改變音調和節奏**

② **腹式發聲法**：為了在演說時，讓聲音傳到遠處，必須使用利用橫隔膜振動的**腹式呼吸法**。

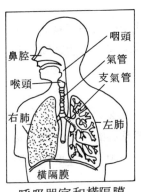

呼吸器官和橫隔膜

橫隔膜是位於腹腔和胸腔之間的肉膜，上面與心臟、肺，下面與胃、脾臟、肝臟等器官相接，由橫隔膜神經控制伸縮，可幫助肺的呼吸。

腹式呼吸的方法：**深吸一口氣使肚子鼓起**。由於橫隔膜往下降，肺就充滿了空氣，此時腹部臟器被下降的橫隔膜所壓迫，腹壁會往外撐，腹部因而鼓起。接下來便是**把吸入的空氣吐出來**。大多的男性，尤其在大聲說話時，自然就會使用腹式呼吸法。但小孩子或女性，呼吸時通常只把胸部挺出來（此為胸式呼吸），橫隔膜並沒有振動，而進入肺臟的空氣也不多，因此發不出宏亮的聲音。而演說時，應該利用腹部呼吸法。在練習腹式呼吸時，有幾點必須注意：

(a) 首先緩緩地深吸一口氣，使肚子鼓起，然後吐氣，使肚子瘻回。

(b) 第二，吐氣可配合**節拍**。用**吸、吸、吐、吐、吐**這種「二吸三吐」的拍子來進行。

(c) 第三，吐氣時就像吹熄蠟燭一樣，臉頰不必鼓起，只要慢慢把氣吐出來即可。

接下來再舉二、三個可就近練習的方法。

(a) 仰臥，在自己的肚子上放一本書，然後呼吸。使書本上下**振動**，做空氣出入腹部的練習。

(b) 面向牆壁而站，身體距離牆壁約 **30 cm**。一手拿著 5 cm 平方的薄紙按在牆壁上。深深吸一口氣，然後向薄紙吐氣。如果手離開，紙不會掉下來的話，再慢慢拉長自己與牆壁的距離。

(c) 這是任何地方都可以做的練習。先吸氣讓肚子中充滿空氣，然後嘴唇微閉把氣慢慢吐出來，再計算全部吐出氣所需要的時間。反覆練習將時間拉長。

③ **演講時的句重音**：*sentence stress*（句重音）是句子中有重要意義單字上的重音。我們在講國語時，對有重要意義的字都會加重語氣，可見這是任何語言都有的現象。句重音經常隨著句中單字重要性的**變動**而改變，不過句重音的一般規則如下：

(a) 在英語的詞類中，可分為有單獨意思的內容字，和表示文法構造的機能字二種。只要不是特別強調，句重音通常都落在**內容字**上。內容字有**名詞、動詞、形容詞、副詞、指示代名詞、疑問代名詞、不定代名詞、所有代名詞、感歎詞**。

(b) **文法上強調的字**，同時也是句重音所在。如：

It was *she* that talked with him yesterday.
I *did* see her yesterday.

(c) 因意義和習慣用法，句重音有時會落在 be 動詞上。如：

Who *are* you？

What *is* it？

Here you *are*.

除了自己想特別**強調**、**重要**的部分或需要特別注入**感情**的地方，原則上按照以上三個規則來加句重音。

④ **講台上的注意事項**：發表演說的過程，應該是從司儀宣佈演說者的姓名，演說者從座位上站起來時就已經算是開始了。等到演說者講完後，坐回自己的座位後才算結束。

到了台上演講的位置後，不要立刻展開演說，最好**停頓二、三秒鐘**才開始。結束演講時也一樣，先停頓二、三秒鐘再離開講台。如果碰到一下子想不起接著要講些什麼的情形時，先不要著急，以自然的姿勢靜靜地**凝視**著觀衆，努力去回想所要講的內容。想起來之後，再自然地接著講下去。最好不要伸舌頭、看天花板、看鞋子或搔頭摸耳，也不必向聽衆說 " *I am sorry.* " 這句話。

　　如何捕捉聽衆的眼神，與演講是否生動有極大的關聯。一般人在與人交談時，都會從注視著對方的眼神，來判斷對方瞭解自己談話內容的程度。但演說時聽衆的人數很多，眼睛必須**來回往左邊、正面、右邊看。**如果可能的話，眼睛可以盯著聽衆中的某一位，這樣可以使心情放輕鬆，有助於自己的演說。

　　此外，演講時的姿勢和動作要**自然**，並且要能配合演講的內容。從演講開始到結束，老是同一個姿勢，會顯得很不自然，而且會引起聽衆的焦躁不安。因此，首先必須採取**自然的**姿勢，應該讓雙手自然地垂在腿側，輕鬆地站立，身體不要左右晃動，也不要把雙手按在講桌上，彎著身體演講，這會讓聽衆覺得你很蠻橫。

Chapter
2

聯誼場合致詞
Ceremonial
Speeches

Unit 1
Greeting Newcomers

● A Sample Speech ●

I am Jason Lee, president of this company.

First, I would like to extend a sincere welcome to you all.

As you know, our company is one of the **big names** and has a long tradition. I think you must be proud of being part of such a great company. But we cannot afford to depend on tradition alone. We need **new blood** like you to bring us new ideas, new knowledge, and new insights.

I would like to welcome you once again, and from today, let us begin to work together.

ADVICE

要做演說或致詞時，請先回憶一下每篇演講稿的基本內容：①開頭②本論③結尾。在這裏開頭先做個簡單的自我介紹，報上姓名和職稱，再陳述歡迎之意。在本論中談及一、二個主旨，結尾則重述歡迎之意。依此三段公式法，你也可以寫一篇模範演講稿。

歡迎新進人員

● 演說實例 ●

我是本公司的董事長李傑森。

首先，我誠摯地歡迎各位來到本公司。

就如各位所知，本公司聲名卓越，歷史悠久。我想，各位能成為這種大公司的一份子，一定也感到很光榮。但是，光憑傳統是不夠的，我們還需要像各位這樣的新血，給我們帶來新觀念，新知識，以及新的洞察力。

我再度歡迎各位。從今天起，讓我們一起攜手合作吧!

** president 〔ˈprɛzədənt〕 *n.* 董事長；總經理
extend 〔ɪkˈstɛnd〕 *v.* 給與　　sincere 〔sɪnˈsɪr〕 *adj.* 誠摯的
big name 知名的人或事　　afford 〔əˈford ; əˈfɔrd〕 *v.* 力足以；能
insight 〔ˈɪnˌsaɪt〕 *n.* 洞察力

Useful Expressions

對新進職員的歡迎辭

1. I am excited to see so many young and energetic faces.

   見到這麼多年輕又精力充沛的面孔，我覺得很高興。

2. The hope and ambition of young people is refreshing.

   年輕人的希望和抱負讓人覺得精神一振。

3. I am sure you *are* all well *equipped with* knowledge.

   我相信你們都具備豐富的專業知識。

4. Welcome to Star City Electric.

   歡迎加入星城電子。

5. I am very pleased to welcome you all.

   能夠來歡迎各位，我非常高興。

6. I am very happy that you will be working with us.

   你們將和我們一起工作，我覺得很高興。

7. Welcome to *the sales department* !

   歡迎加入銷售部！

8. We want to welcome you to *the planning department*.

   我們歡迎你加入企畫部。

9. We are glad that you'll be part of our department.

   我們很高興你們將成爲本部的一份子。

** energetic〔ɛnɚˋdʒɛtɪk〕 *adj*. 活躍的　　ambition〔æmˋbɪʃən〕 *n*. 野心
refreshing〔rɪˋfrɛʃɪŋ〕 *adj*. 有精神的　　equip〔ɪˋkwɪp〕 *v*. 使學得

激勵新進職員

1. Our company needs young people with new and professional ideas.

   我們公司需要有新點子及專業技術的年輕人。

2. "Working smart" is more important than "working hard."

   「聰明地工作」比「拼命地工作」更爲重要。

3. I want you to learn to think creatively.

   我希望你們能學著使思考富有創意。

4. It's about time you *put* what you've learned *into practice*.

   該是你們把所學付諸實用的時候了！

5. I want you to work for yourself, and for the well-being of the society.

   我希望你們能爲自己而工作，爲整個社會的福利而工作。

** professional 〔prə'fɛʃənl〕 *adj.* 專業的
smart 〔smɑrt〕 *adj.* 伶俐的；精明的
put ~ into practice 將～付諸實行　　well-being 〔wɛl'biɪŋ〕 *n.* 福利

● 演說小教室 ●

在眾人面前演講最擔心的即是會**怯場**，克服的方法之一，就是告訴自己：「緊張是自然的反應;正常人都會如此。」。另一個方法，就是在演說前和旁邊的人**說說笑笑**。爲了避免一緊張喉嚨會乾，而說不出話來，可一邊喝點水或果汁，一邊和身旁的人閒話家常，讓舌頭、嘴唇和臉部肌肉做熱身運動。如此一來，在麥克風前就可流暢地演說了。

Unit 2
Receiving Foreign Guests

● A Sample Speech ●

We are proud and honored to have such a distinguished group of guests come **all the way** from the United States to visit our company.

Our staff and employees will **do their best** to make your visit comfortable and worthwhile. Today, they will introduce you to our newly-built plant and research center. Please do not hesitate to ask any questions you may have.

I want to extend my warmest welcome to all of you, and sincerely hope that your visit here will be worthwhile and meaningful.

ADVICE

歡迎遠道而來的貴賓，首先要對他們千里迢迢特地來訪表示謝意，並表示自己對他們的來訪十分重視。因此這篇演講的開頭部分就是重心所在。而在本論中則要提到整個訪問的行程，必要時還可以介紹一下負責接待這些外賓的人員。結尾則再次表達歡迎之意。

迎接外賓

● 演說實例 ●

　　各位貴賓，從美國遠道而來參觀本公司，我們感到非常榮幸。

　　本公司員工一定會盡力使各位在訪問期間，旣舒適又充實。今天，他們會帶領各位，去參觀我們新建的工廠以及研究中心。各位如果有任何問題，請別客氣，儘量提出來。

　　我向各位致上最誠摯的歡迎，並衷心希望各位在此地的訪問旣充實又有意義。

** honored 〔'ɑnəd〕 *adj*. 可敬的
distinguished 〔dɪ'stɪŋgwɪʃ〕 *adj*. 卓著的；優秀的
staff 〔stæf, stɑf〕 *n*. 員工　employee 〔ɪm'plɔɪ·i,͵ɪmplɔɪ'·i〕 *n*. 雇員
worthwhile 〔'wɝθhwaɪl〕 *adj*. 值得做的
hesitate 〔'hɛzə͵tet〕 *v*. 遲疑

Useful Expressions

感謝遠道而來

1. We would like to thank you for coming to visit our company.

感謝各位前來參觀本公司。

2. It is a great pleasure having you here.

各位能夠前來，真是我們的一大榮幸。

3. I am pleased to meet such an interesting group of people.

我很高興能遇見像各位這麼有趣的人。

4. It is an honor and a privelege to receive a visit from such a distinguished group. (*formal*)

能夠接待各位貴賓來訪，真是我們的榮幸。(正式)

5. Thank you for coming **all the way** to Taiwan to visit us.

感謝各位大老遠來到台灣，參觀我們的公司。

歡迎來訪者的問候語

1. I want to welcome you all.

歡迎各位。

2. Let me cordially welcome you to our company.

我熱誠地歡迎各位前來本公司。

3. I would like to extend a warm welcome to you all.

我要向各位致上誠摯的歡迎。

4. Welcome to ABC Electronics.

歡迎光臨 ABC 電子公司。

＊＊ privilege〔'prɪvɪlɪdʒ〕*n.* 榮幸　　***all the way*** 一路上；遙遠
cordially〔'kɔrdʒəlɪ〕*adv.* 誠摯地

與訪問行程有關的例句

1. We will *do our best* to make your visit a comfortable one.

我們將盡力使各位在訪問期間舒適愉快。

2. Please *feel free* to ask us any questions you may have.

如果有任何問題，請各位別客氣，儘管提出來。

3. Today we would like to show you around our headquarters.

今天，我們想帶領各位參觀我們的總部。

4. Today you will be introduced to the information processing center.

今天，我們將向你們介紹本公司的資料處理中心。

** feel free 不必擔心；請別客氣

● 演說小教室 ●

　　當有人請你用英語演講時，你的演講稿應該一開始就用**英文寫**。剛開始，可用中文寫下①**開頭**②**本論**③**結尾**三段的大綱，再參考本書中的例句，試寫一篇演講稿。如果將中文草稿直接譯成英文稿，是很難寫出純正的英語演講稿的。寫完之後，別忘了大聲朗讀一遍，看看是否通順，有無拗口的字或音。如果可能的話，找個外國人聽你唸一遍，幫你糾正發音及語調。

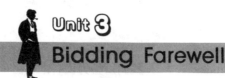

Unit 3
Bidding Farewell

● A Sample Speech ●

As you know, Mr. Jones will soon be leaving us to become the director of the Los Angeles branch.

I am very happy that he has been promoted. For the five years Mr. Jones has been with us, his ability and dedication have always been a source of pride to us. His absence from this office will be a great loss.

However, it will definitely be a great gain for the Los Angeles office. Mr. Jones, we are going to miss you very much, and we **wish you the very best of luck** in your future.

ADVICE

歡送離職人員的致詞，免不了要讚美對方的優點及對公司的貢獻，並陳述大家的懷念與祝福。若歡送的對象是因升遷(promote) 或調職(transfer)而離開，則在開始就要點出，而且別忘了要加上祝賀的話。

歡送離職人員

● 演說實例 ●

　　就如你們所知，瓊斯先生即將離開我們，前往洛杉磯分公司擔任主管。

　　對於他的高陞，我感到很高興。瓊斯先生跟我們在一起的這五年當中，他的才能以及他盡心盡力的精神一直是我們的驕傲。他離開這裏，將是我們的一大損失。

　　不過，這對洛杉磯分公司而言，絕對是一大利益，瓊斯先生，我們會非常想念你；同時，我們預祝你未來充滿好運。

** branch〔bræntʃ〕*n.* 分公司　　dedication〔͵dɛdə'keʃən〕*n.* 奉獻
absence〔'æbsn̩s〕*n.* 缺席
definitely〔'dɛfənɪtlɪ〕*adv.* 明確地；絕對地

Useful Expressions

▌惜別用語

1. We are very sad to say goodbye to Mr. Johnson. — 要跟强生先生說再見，我們感到非常難過。

2. It is very unfortunate that Mr. Douglas will be leaving us. — 道格拉斯先生卽將離開我們，眞是令人遺憾。

3. I regret to announce Mr. Davis' resignation. (*formal*) — 我很遺憾，要宣佈大衞斯先生的離職。(正式)

4. We are going to miss you, Tom. (*informal*) — 我們會想念你的，湯姆。(非正式)

▌提到調職之處

1. Mr. Brown has been promoted to manager of our U.S. branch. — 布朗先生已經榮陞我們美國分公司經理。

2. Mr. Hoffman will **be transferred to** New York next month. — 霍夫曼先生下個月將調到紐約去。

▌讚美離職者

1. We're going to miss her smiling face. — 我們會想念她微笑的臉。

2. We were fortunate to have worked with him for so many years. — 我們能夠跟他共事那麼多年，眞是幸運。

** unfortunate 〔ʌnˋfɔrtʃənɪt〕 *adj.* 令人遺憾的；不幸的
announce 〔əˋnaʊns〕 *v.* 宣布　resignation 〔͵rɛzɪgˋneʃən〕 *n.* 辭職
transfer 〔trænsˋfɝ〕 *v.* 調職；移轉

3. We enjoyed every minute that   我們和您一起工作的每一分、
we worked with you.   每一秒，都十分愉快。

● 演說小教室 ●

如果是在歡送**同事或上司退休**（ retirement ）的場合上致詞，最好採取較**正式**的語氣，因為對方的身份多屬德高望重型，而且態度也以莊重為宜。

It was a surprise to learn of your retirement. We didn't expect you to retire so soon. Your leadership and company will surely be missed by everyone here. You have been an inspiration to all of us. You have been **a hard act to follow**.

We know you now have more important things to pursue and we respect your decision very much. We wish you all the best in the world though.

Thank you for all the good times **as well as** the bad, for we have learned a lot from you. We **take our hats off to you**. Good luck and God bless your soul.

知道您退休的消息真是令人驚訝，因為我們沒料到您這麼快就要退休了。在這兒的每一個人都會想念您的領導和陪伴。您不僅鼓勵我們，也是我們模範的楷模。

我們知道您現在有更多重要的事待辦，我們都非常尊重您的決定。祝福您萬事如意。

感謝您，不論在順境或逆境中，我們都向您學習了許多。我們向您致敬，也祝您幸運。願上帝保佑您。

** retirement〔rɪ'taɪrmənt〕*n.* 退休
  inspiration〔͵ɪnspə'reʃən〕*n.* 啟示；鼓勵者
  pursue〔pə'su, pə'sɪu〕*v.* 追求
  take one's hat off to sb. 對某人表示敬意

Unit 4
Birthday Party

● A Sample Speech ●

I'm sure everybody will agree with me that Bob has always been a great boss. I have never met a person who is as understanding and patient as Bob.

We have thrown this birthday party not only to celebrate your birthday, Bob, but also to express our gratitude for your thoughtful leadership. So thank you from all of us.

Happy birthday, Bob, and many happy returns!

ADVICE

在國外，部屬主動爲上司安排生日宴會，是撇開公事和上司建立友誼的好機會。因爲是較輕鬆且非正式的場合，所以不需要生硬的介紹詞。如果過生日的是女性的話，適時的一句："We all wonder how you always look so young and elegant!"（我們都很想知道，爲什麼妳總是那麼優雅年輕。）將使對方受用無窮。

生日宴會

● 演説實例 ●

　　我相信大家都會同意，鮑伯一直是個很棒的上司。我從來沒有遇見像鮑伯這麼體恤他人又有耐心的人。

　　鮑伯，我們舉辦這個生日宴會，不只是要慶祝你的生日而已，我們還要對你體貼的領導表示感激。我們全體謝謝你。

　　生日快樂，鮑伯，並祝你福如東海，壽比南山。

** patient〔'peʃənt〕*adj.* 有耐心的　　　throw〔θro〕*v.* 舉行宴會
　 express〔ɪk'sprɛs〕*v.* 表示　　　gratitude〔'grætətjud〕*n.* 感謝

Useful Expressions

生日賀辭

1. Happy birthday, John, and best wishes in the years to come.

   生日快樂，約翰，並祝你在未來的歲月中，一切順利。

2. I would like to wish you a happy fiftieth birthday — may you have fifty more!

   祝你五十歲生日快樂——並祝你還有五十年。

3. I would like to *propose a toast* to Mr. Stevenson on his sixtieth birthday. (*formal*)

   史帝文先生六十大壽，我提議舉杯敬他。(非正式)

4. I wish you many *happy returns of the day*.

   祝您福如東海，壽比南山。

5. We all wish you the very best of luck, health, and wealth.

   我們祝你萬事如意，身體健康，財源滾滾！

提到生日者的年齡

1. Happy birthday, Mr. Wilson. You are indeed *seventy-five years young*.

   生日快樂，威爾森先生。你七十五歲，却老當益壯啊！

2. Confucius once said, "one stands *on his own* at thirty." Well, John, I'm sure he would be impressed with you if he were here.

   子曰:「三十而立。」嗯,約翰,如果孔子在這裏,我相信他一定會對你印象深刻。

** propose 〔prə'poz〕 *v.* 提議   toast 〔tost〕 *n.* 敬酒
   impress 〔ɪm'prɛs〕 *v.* 使印象深刻

3. They say that after forty, we paint our faces from the inside. Well, Tom, you're looking better than ever.

人家說，一個人在四十歲以後，他的內在會表現在臉上。嗯，湯姆，你看起來再好不過了。

4. It is really wonderful for all of us to grow older together and work together under your leadership.

對我們而言，能在您的領導之下，一同工作，一同成長，將是件愉快的事。

5. To all of us, you are always *in your twenties*.

對我們而言，妳看起來總是二十幾歲而已。

6. We all want to know your secret of staying young.

我們都很想知道妳青春永駐的秘訣。

** *in one's twenties* 在某人 20 幾歲的階段

● 演說小教室 ●

要讓每次的致詞演說都成為完美的演出，就必須好好研究一下 stance（**立足點**）的問題。在演說時，「**演說者**」（speaker）、「**聽眾**」（audience）和「**話題**」（topic of speech）是判斷 stance 的三個要素。例如，對昇遷的上司發表賀詞時，是要採取他是上司的語氣，還是當他是慈祥的長輩呢？基於這種立足點的不同，致詞的內容當然就不同了。因此，在擬稿之前，必須先設定好自己的立足點並了解 speaker、audience 和 topic of speech 三者間的互動關係。

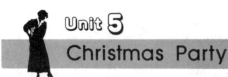

Unit 5
Christmas Party

● A Sample Speech ●

On behalf of our entire company, I want to thank you for inviting us to such an enjoyable Christmas party.

We really enjoyed the delicious food and excellent wine. Also, the music was perfect, so if I were a better dancer I could have enjoyed the party **twice as much.**

I enjoyed meeting and talking to you, and sharing the time together. I hope we will be able to maintain this good relationship and make next year another great one together.

Thank you again for the wonderful party. We had a great time.

ADVICE

被外國客戶邀請參加他們公司舉辦的聖誕舞會（Christmas party）時，只吃飯喝酒、跳舞，然後就離去,是很不禮貌的。離開前應該說些感謝的話，若能順便提到繼續維持兩家公司間的友好關係，那就更圓滿了。此外，別忘了聖誕舞會是輕鬆愉快的場合，所以致詞應簡短、幽默，配合歡樂的氣氛。

耶誕晚會

● 演說實例 ●

　　我代表我們公司全體，感謝你們邀請我們來參加這麼愉快的耶誕舞會。

　　我們真的很喜歡你們的佳餚美酒。還有，音樂也棒極了。如果我的舞跳得好一點的話，我的愉快就更要加倍了。

　　我很高興見到你們，跟你們聊天，並和你們分享這段時光。我希望我們能夠維持這種良好的關係，共同再創美好的明年。

　　再度謝謝你們這個美妙的舞會，我們玩得很開心。

** *on behalf of* ~　代表~　　delicious〔dɪˈlɪʃəs〕*adj.* 美味的
maintain〔menˈten〕*v.* 保持

Useful Expressions

感謝邀請

1. It was very kind *of* you to invite us.

   你們邀請我們，真是對我們太好了。

2. It is a great pleasure to be invited here. (*formal*)

   能夠被邀請前來此地，真是一大榮幸。（正式）

3. *Thanks for* inviting me tonight, John.

   謝謝你今晚邀請我，約翰。

舞會結束時的謝辭

1. It was a great pleasure getting to know you.

   能夠認識你們，真是非常愉快。

2. I greatly appreciate your hospitality.

   我非常感激你們的慇懃招待。

3. I enjoyed it very much. Thanks for everything.

   我玩得很開心，謝謝。

4. I am deeply grateful for this nice arrangement, and I enjoyed every minute of it.

   非常感謝這次完美的安排，我每一分，每一秒都很愉快。

5. It was such a lot of fun.

   實在非常好玩。

6. I enjoyed everything, and *above all*, I enjoyed talking to and getting to know you.

   我玩得很愉快，更愉快的是能夠認識各位並和各位聊天。

** appreciate 〔ə'priʃɪ,et〕 *v.* 感激　hospitality 〔hɑspɪ'tælətɪ〕 *n.* 慇懃款待
grateful 〔'gretfl〕 *adj.* 感謝的　*above all* 最重要的是

提及兩家公司的關係

1. I hope we will be able to continue our close cooperation.

我希望我們能夠繼續維持密切的合作關係。

2. I hope next year's *sales growth*
will be even better.

我希望明年的銷售成長將會更好。

3. I hope we will get together again
next year.

希望明年我們能夠再聚。

4. I hope we will have another
great year.

希望我們明年的業績會更好。

5. I hope our *harmonious business
relationship* will keep us together next year too.

希望我們事業上的和諧關係，能讓我們明年再聚。

** cooperation 〔ko,ɑpə'reʃən〕 *n.* 合作
harmonious 〔hɑr'monɪəs〕 *adj.* 和諧的

● 演說小教室 ●

　　初次上台致詞的人常有個毛病，那就是將背好的稿子，照本宣科的唸出來。這種唸課本式的單調語氣，不僅對聽眾而言是種折磨，有時反而會因此影響當時的氣氛，造成反效果。但要如何才能把稿子「背」得不留痕跡，像平常說話一樣呢？以下有三個原則：

(1) 注意句與句之間的**停頓**，不要讓自己因唸長句而喘不過氣來。

(2) 分辨**語調**的高低及**語氣**的轉折處。

(3) 關於發音是否標準，與其求好心切，失却信心，不如量力而為，以「**可以接受**」（acceptable）為目的即可。

Unit 6
The Year-end Party

● A Sample Speech ●

We want to thank all the people here for **taking the time out** of your busy schedule to come to our year-end party.

Tonight we are very fortunate to have our friends from Krypton Computer Company with us to celebrate the year-end festivities together. We hope you will all have a good time.

Now, let us **propose a toast** on this happy occasion. (After all the cups and glasses have been filled) Here's to Krypton!

ADVICE

邀請外國友人參加公司的年終尾牙（year-end party），除了聯誼的目的之外，還可以讓他們體驗一下傳統中國老板慰勞員工的方式。此時的致詞以簡短，非正式為主。內容也只是向出席者道謝，介紹客人來賓及各種餘興節目而已。當然也不免舉杯共祝一番。

年終尾牙

● 演說實例 ●

我們要感謝所有在座各位，在百忙中抽空來參加我們
的年終聚會。

今晚，我們非常榮幸，能夠請到克里普頓電腦公司的
朋友們，和我們一起參加年終的慶祝活動。希望你們都能
盡興。

現在，在這個愉快的時刻，讓我們一起舉杯祝賀。（
在所有杯子都斟滿之後）敬克里普頓公司。

** schedule〔'skɛdʒʊl〕*n.* 時間表　　year-end party 尾牙
　　festivity〔fɛs'tɪvətɪ〕*n.* 慶祝　　occasion〔ə'keʒən〕*n.* 場合；時機

Useful Expressions

向來賓致謝

1. I would like to thank you for coming **all the way** out here.

我要謝謝各位大老遠來到這裏。

2. We are so glad you could be with us at this year-end party.

各位能夠來參加這個尾牙聚會，我們感到很高興。

3. Let me say how happy we are to have you all here.

你們各位能夠前來，我們真是太高興了。

4. We appreciate your **taking time out from your busy schedule** to be with us tonight.

各位今晚在百忙之中抽空前來，我們非常感激。

5. I am so glad to have you here.

你們來了，我太高興了。

有關年終聚會

1. We will **do our best** to make this evening an enjoyable one.

我們將盡力使今晚充滿歡樂。

2. If there is anything you'd like, please let us know.

如果各位有任何需要，請告訴我們。

3. Later on, some of our employees will entertain us with "Gong Show" performances.

等一會兒，我們的員工會表演一些餘興節目。

4. Let's forget our troubles and have a great time together.

讓我們忘掉煩惱，一起共渡美好時光。

** **Gong Show** 原為美國電視節目名稱，現成為餘興節目的代名詞。
performance 〔pə'fɔrməns〕 *n.* 表演

5. The Year-end party, or what we call "Wei-ya", is a part held by the boss to thank his employees for their hard working during the year.

年終聚會，或我們所稱的「尾牙」是老闆為慰勞員工們今年的辛勤工作而舉辦的宴會。

敬酒勸食用語

1. Let me *propose a toast to* a prosperous business.

讓我們舉杯預祝生意興隆。

2. Here's to each of us.

讓我們為自己乾杯。

3. *Let's drink to* Johnson Company and ABC Electric.

我們來敬強生公司和ABC電子公司。

4. Three cheers for our successful business!

讓我們來歡呼三次，祝我們公司順利成功。

5. We hope you will have a good time sampling Chinese cuisine.

希望你們能好好享受中國美食。

** prosperous〔'prɑspərəs〕*adj.* 興隆的　　cheer〔tʃɪr〕*n.* 喝采
cuisine〔kwɪ'zin〕*n.* 烹飪

● 演說小教室 ●

　　如果大家推選你擔任晚會餘興節目的主持人；你也可以用英文好好表現一番。雖說主持人的工作只是讓來賓摸彩，按照號碼分送獎品而已，但其中如何掌握現場氣氛，並讓在場的外國友人有參與感，卻是需要一些技巧。例如在抽獎前，可先說" Let's see who will get third prize." 然後停頓一下，讓大家凝神靜聽，最後再大聲說" Here we go ! "，發表得獎人名單。

Unit 7
The New Year Party

● A Sample Speech ●

Happy New Year, everybody.

I am very happy to see all of you here to celebrate the arrival of the new year. **In particular,** I am delighted to have Mr. Williams and Mr. Richardson from the United Electric Company here with us. Mr. Williams and Mr. Richardson, I really appreciate your presence here tonight.

I hope you will have a good time tonight, and I wish every one of you a very happy new year. **Let's all have fun!**

ADVICE ⌒.

公司舉辦的新年酒會（ New Year party ）也可以邀請外國客戶來參加。主持人的工作就是發表 opening speech 。在演講中當然要感謝客人的參加，但美酒佳餚當前，演講內容應該儘量縮短，而且最好能夠掀起歡樂的氣氛，因此開頭的"Happy New year, everyboday！"和結尾的" Let's all have fun."要大聲地說出來，不要覺得不好意思。

新年酒會

● 演說實例 ●

　　大家新年快樂！

　　我很高興看見各位在新年來臨時，一起在這裏慶祝。尤其，聯合電子公司的威廉斯先生和理查森先生能夠前來，更是令我高興。威廉斯先生、理查森先生，我真得很感激你們今晚蒞臨。

　　我希望各位今晚能夠玩得愉快，並祝每一個人新年快樂。大家盡情地玩吧！

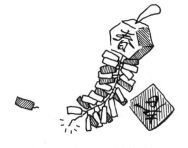

** arrival〔əˋraɪvḷ〕*n.* 到達　　*in particular* 特別地
appreciate〔əˋpriʃɪ͵et〕*v.* 感激

Useful Expressions

新年賀詞

1. I wish you the best of luck in the new year.

我祝各位新年行大運。

2. I hope the new year will bring you lots of luck and happiness.

我祝大家新年充滿好運及快樂。

3. I want to give you my best wishes for the new year.

我要把最誠摯的新年祝福獻給各位。

關於新的一年

1. The new year is a time to *start over* and *begin anew*.

新年是新的開始。

2. Let's see if we can *live up to* our New Year's resolutions.

我們要看看自己能不能達成新年時下定決心要做的事。

3. The New Year's party gives us a chance to strengthen our relationship.

新年酒會給我們一個加強彼此關係的機會。

勸食用語

1. Help yourself. Don't be shy!

自己動手,別不好意思!

2. Eat and drink *to your heart's content*.

請儘量吃、儘量喝。

** anew 〔ə'n(j)u〕 *adv.* 重新　　*live up to* 達到預期標準
resolution 〔ˌrezə'ljuʃən〕 *n.* 決心　　*to one's heart's content* 隨某人所喜

3. Let's have a good time. 讓我們玩個痛快吧！

4. Please enjoy the traditional New Year's dishes. 請享用傳統的新年佳餚。

5. I hope you will enjoy this Chinese-style New Year's party. 希望你們喜歡這種中國式的新年酒會。

● 演說小教室 ●

結束酒會時，也可以做個簡短的 closing speech，一方面總結各種餘興活動，一方面再度感謝賓客的蒞臨。

May I have your attention please?

Well, looks like you've been having a good time drinking, eating and talking to each other. But I'm afraid we have to wind up this party now.

I am so glad that we have **started** the new year successfully **with** this party tonight. You might want to stay here longer, but we **are running out of time**, **and also running out of** food and drinks, unfortunately.

I want to thank you all for coming to the party, and I wish you a happy new year again.

各位來賓！請看我這裏，好嗎？

嗯，看起來各位似乎都已酒酣耳熱，聊得很愉快。可是，恐怕我們現在必須要結束這次酒會了。

很高興能以今晚的酒會成功地迎接新的一年。你們可能希望再多待一會兒，不過，時間已晚，菜餚也吃得差不多了。

在此謝謝各位來賓的光臨，再次祝大家新年快樂。

** attention〔əˈtɛnʃən〕*n.* 注意　　*wind up* 結束
run out of 用完；耗盡

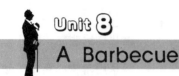

Unit 8
A Barbecue

• A Sample Speech •

Good evening, and welcome to my residence.

I am very happy that so many of you could come. Last night I was a little worried about rain, but as it **turned out**, the weather is beautiful.

It's really nice to see you in a different and informal setting like this. I hope this party will give us all a good opportunity to get to know one another better.

I'm going to barbecue some chicken, and Mr. Chen will take care of the pork and beef. We have a variety of food and drinks. So **help yourself** and have fun !

ADVICE

美商公司的上司，常會利用假日，邀請公司職員到家裏來舉行烤肉聚餐（barbecue），以促進彼此的感情。這是極美國化且不拘形式的社交方式，且多半在戶外的庭院中舉行，參加者可以輕裝前往。身爲主人的開場白，必然是先歡迎大家，重要的還是說明在什麼時候、什麼地方可以吃到食物和飲料。

烤肉聚餐

● 演說實例 ●

大家晚安，歡迎到我家來。

這麼多人光臨，我很高興。昨天晚上我還有點耽心會下雨。不過結果天氣很好。

能夠在這樣一個不同，又非正式的場合看見各位，真是太好了。我希望這次宴會能提供我們一個更了解彼此的好機會。

我來烤雞肉，陳先生則負責豬肉和牛肉。我們有多種食物和飲料，請各位自行取用，並請大家盡情地玩。

** residence〔ˈrɛzədəns〕*n.* 住處　　setting〔ˈsɛtɪŋ〕*n.* 場合；環境
opportunity〔ˌɑpɚˈt(j)unətɪ〕*n.* 機會
barbecue〔ˈbɑrbɪˌkju〕*v.* 烤肉　　variety〔vəˈraɪətɪ〕*n.* 多種

Useful Expressions

█ 開場白

1. It's nice to see everybody.　　　見到各位眞好。

2. Well, you look hungry, so I'll
   try to make it short.

   嗯，你們看起來都餓了，所
   以我盡量簡短一點。

3. Well, I guess everyone is here,
   and I'm sure *you're dying to eat*.

   嗯，我想大家都來了，而且
   我相信你們都餓壞了。

█ 閒聊天氣用語

1. I'm glad it's *cleared up*. I guess
   the weatherman was right for once.

   我很高興天氣放晴了。天氣
   預報總算對了一次。

2. It's a beautiful day, so enjoy the
   sunshine.

   今天天氣很好，請大家盡情
   享受陽光。

3. Too bad it's raining. I hope it'll
   clear up soon.

   下雨了，眞糟糕！我希望很
   快就會放晴。

4. We are having a beautiful day.　　今天的天氣非常好。

█ 提及餐會的目的

1. I hope you have a chance to get
   to know each other.

   我希望各位能有個機會了解
   彼此。

2. This is a great opportunity to *get
   acquainted with* one another.

   這是各位彼此熟悉的大好機
   會。

** weatherman 〔'wɛðɚ,mæn〕 *n.* 天氣預報員
　　acquaint 〔ə'kwent〕 *v.* 熟識　*get acquainted with* ～ 與～熟識

3. Enjoy the barbecue, beer, and
   wine, but don't forget to enjoy
   meeting one another.

好好地享用這些烤肉、啤酒
和美酒吧！不過也別忘了互
相認識一番喔！

● 演說小教室 ●

非正式的聚會上通常沒有 closing speech（閉幕詞），賓
客多三三兩兩各自離去，但有時也有主人宣佈散會的情形。在
閉幕詞中必須提到**幫助籌備宴會的人，**不要忘了感謝他們的辛勞。

May have your attention, please?

Well, I guess I have to say the party is coming
to a close. I am very happy that you all seem to
have enjoyed talking and getting to know each other.
I hope the barbecue was good enough and everybody
has eaten enough.

I want to mention that Mr. & Mrs. Chen helped
a great deal to prepare the food, drinks, and other things
for the party. **So please give them a big hand.**

I want to thank you again for coming, and hope
you'll enjoy the rest of the weekend. **I'm looking forward
to** seeing you refreshed and revitalized on Monday.

各位，請看我這裏，好嗎？

嗯，我想這次聚會要告個段落了，非常高興你們都能彼此認識，而
且談得很愉快。希望大家喜歡今天的烤肉，而且都能飽餐一頓。

我要提一下陳先生夫婦，他們幫忙準備聚會的食物、飲料和其它東
西。所以，請給他們一次愛的鼓勵。

再次謝謝各位的參加，祝大家周末愉快。希望星期一能看到各位精
神飽滿，容光煥發。

** ***come to a close*** 結束　mention〔'mɛnʃən〕*v.* 提及
a big hand 拍手喝采　　***look forward to*** 期待
refreshed〔rɪ'frɛʃt〕*adj.* 有精神的
revitalized〔ri'vaɪtl͵aɪz〕*adj.* 恢復生氣的

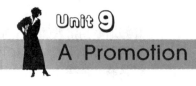

Unit 9
A Promotion

• A Sample Speech •

A **Congratulations**, Mr. Hoffman, **on** your promotion to managing director of the personnel department. Under your directorship, I am sure the department will grow even stronger and more closely united.

Also, **I want to take this opportunity to** thank you for being our section director. Needless to say, you have always been a great boss, and I'm sure you will make an even greater director in the personnel department.

B I want to say congratulations to you, Jim, for your promotion to **sales manager**. You have been a great colleague as well as a good friend. And I am proud of you.

Gook luck, Jim, and come drop by our office any time.

ADVICE

祝賀上司昇遷的演講中，不要忘了感謝上司多年來的照顧。至於祝賀同事時，可以從好朋友的立場，表示他的昇遷是你的驕傲。上司或同事高昇時，常會舉辦慶祝會。其中A是對上司，B是對同事昇遷的演說。

祝賀升遷

● 演說實例 ●

A 賀夫曼先生，恭喜你升為人事部經理。我相信今後人事部在您的管理之下，必然更團結，成長更穩健。

同時，我也要籍這個機會，感謝您過去身為本部門的經理。不用說，您是一位好上司，而且我深信在人事部，您將會是一位更好的經理。

B 吉姆，我要恭喜你升為業務部經理。你一直是位好同事、好朋友，我以你為榮。

吉姆，祝你好運。歡迎有空常來我們辦公室坐坐。

** congratulation 〔kən‚grætʃəˈleʃən〕 *n.* 祝賀
   promotion 〔prəˈmoʃən〕 *n.* 昇遷　personnel 〔‚pɝsṇˈɛl〕 *n.* 職員；人事
   directorship 〔dəˈrɛktə‚ʃɪp〕 *n.* 管理者（的職位；任期）
   colleague 〔ˈkɑlig〕 *n.* 同事　***drop by*** 順路拜訪

Useful Expressions

祝賀上司陞遷

1. We would like to **congratulate** Mr. Thompson **on** his promotion **to** service manager.

   我們恭賀湯普生先生高陞服務部經理。

2. We were very happy to hear of your promotion to the board.

   我們聽說你高陞為董事，都非常高興。

祝賀同事陞遷

1. Congratulations on your promotion, John. I am very happy for you.

   恭禧你升官了，約翰，我真替你高興。

2. Congratulations, Mary. I hope I can **follow in your footsteps**.

   恭禧妳，瑪麗，希望我也能跟上妳的腳步。

3. Congratulations, Larry. Don't work too hard.

   恭禧啊，賴利，可別累壞了喔！

4. I would be dishonest if I said I was not **envious of** you.

   說我不嫉妒你，那是騙人的。

5. You've set a good example. I'll work hard and get promotion next.

   你已經樹立了好榜樣，我會更加努力以求表現。

** congratulate〔kən'grætʃə,let〕 *v.* 恭喜　　board〔bord,bord〕 *n.* 董事會
footstep〔'fʊt,stɛp〕 *n.* 腳步
dishonest〔dɪs'ɑnɪst〕 *adj.* 不誠實的；騙人的
envious〔'ɛnvɪəs〕 *adj.* 嫉妒的；羨慕的

● 演說小教室 ●

有時昇遷的對象是比自己**地位低**的部屬，這時你的致詞就含有鼓勵的成分。重點在強調部屬的**能力**及職位的**重要性**。

Congratulations, Mr. Jackson, on your promotion to Director of the Taipei liaison office. When I first heard about your promotion, it was no surprise to me, because with your experience, knowledge, and skills in personnel management you will surely be able to fulfill the responsibilities of this important position. The liaison office plays an important role in our company. With your directorship, I am sure it will play an even more important role.

Congratulations again, and I hope you will **enjoy your new post.**

傑克森先生，恭喜你晉升為台北辦事處經理，當我聽到這個消息時，我一點也不驚訝。因為憑你的經驗、知識及人事管理方面的技巧，你應當可以承擔這份重要的職位。本公司十分重視台北辦事處，我相信在你的主持下，它將會發揮更重要的功能。

再次恭喜你，祝你上任愉快。

** liaison〔lie'zɔ〕*n.* 連絡　　*liaison office* 辦事處
post〔post〕*n.* 職位　　fulfill〔fʊl'fɪl〕*v.* 實踐；盡（義務等）
responsibility〔rɪ'spɑnsə'bɪlətɪ〕*n.* 責任

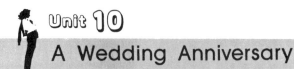

Unit 10
A Wedding Anniversary

• A Sample Speech •

O_n **behalf of** all the employees here tonight, I would like to extend our congratulations to Mr. and Mrs. Johnson on the occasion of their twenty-fifth wedding anniversary.

Traditionally, a gift of silver is given on the twenty-fifth anniversary. We **observe that tradition**, and would like to present a pair of silver cups to honor your marriage. With these cups, I'm sure your marriage will always be **in high spirits** !

Congratulations, Mr. and Mrs. Johnson !

ADVICE

在老闆、上司或重要客戶的結婚周年慶（wedding anniver-sary）上致詞時，除了祝他們圓滿、幸福的婚姻生活外，可以準備與結婚年數有關的禮物，當做發揮幽默感的小道具。

- 結婚一周年　　　　paper anniversary　　（紙婚）
- 結婚五周年　　　　wooden anniversary　（木婚）
- 結婚十周年　　　　tin anniversary　　　（錫婚）
- 結婚十五周年　　　crystal anniversary　（水晶婚）
- 結婚二十周年　　　China anniversary　　（瓷婚）
- 結婚二十五周年　　silver anniversary　　（銀婚）
- 結婚三十周年　　　pearl anniversary　　（珍珠婚）
- 結婚五十周年　　　golden anniversary　（金婚）
- 結婚六十周年　　　diamond anniversary （鑽石婚）

結婚紀念日

● 演說實例 ●

　　今天是強生夫婦結婚二十五週年紀念，我代表今晚在場的所有員工向他們道賀。

　　傳統上，二十五週年要送銀製的禮物，因此，我們遵守傳統，送你們一對銀杯，以表示我們的敬意。有了這對銀杯，我相信你們的婚姻將會永遠幸福愉快。

　　恭禧你們，強生先生、強生太太！

** ***on behalf of*** ~ 代表　　extend〔ɪk'stɛnd〕v. 給與
anniversary〔͵ænə'vɝsərɪ〕n. 週年紀念日　　observe〔əb'zɝv〕v. 遵守
present〔prɪ'zɛnt〕v. 致贈　　***in high spirits*** 生氣勃勃地；心情愉快地

Useful Expressions

來賓的謝辭

1. I am very happy to be invited to your anniversary party.

我很高興能被邀請參加你們的週年宴會。

2. Thank you very much for inviting me to your anniversary party.

非常感謝你們邀請我來參加你們的週年宴會。

3. I am very excited to be a part of this celebration.

我能夠參與這項慶祝活動，感到非常興奮。

4. It is a great honor to be able to join you in celebrating Mr. and Mrs. Smith's 25th wedding anniversary. (*formal*)

能夠跟各位一起慶祝史密斯夫婦結婚二十五週年紀念，真是我的一大榮幸。（正式）

5. I'm very happy for you both. (*informal*)

我真替你們兩位感到高興。（非正式）

頌揚結婚紀念用語

1. ***Congratulations on*** your twenty-fifth wedding anniversary.

恭禧你們結婚二十五週年。

2. Everyone in the department wishes you a happy fiftieth anniversary.

本部門全體人員祝你們五十週年愉快。

3. It is a great pleasure for all of us to celebrate the thirtieth anniversary of Mr. and Mrs. White. (*formal*)

能夠慶祝懷特夫婦結婚三十週年，是我們全體的榮幸。（正式）

** celebration 〔͵sɛlə'breʃən〕 *n.* 慶祝活動

4. Let me say "congratulations" to the happy couple. (*informal*)

我要向這對快樂的佳偶說聲「恭禧」。(非正式)

5. I seriously wish I would be able to learn from President and Mrs. Johnson about the secret of having a happy and enduring marriage.

我真心地希望能向董事長夫婦學習維持幸福永久婚姻的秘訣.

致贈禮物用語

1. We would like to *present* a pair of silver cups *to* you.

我們要送你們一對銀杯。

2. Please accept this silver tray as a token of our esteem.

請接受這個銀盤,它代表我們的敬意。

** seriously 〔'sɪrɪəslɪ〕 *adv*. 認真的;真心的　enduring 〔ɪn'd(j)ʊrɪŋ〕*adj*. 持久的
token 〔'tokən〕 *n*. 象徵　　esteem 〔əs'tim〕 *n*. 尊重;敬意

● 演說小教室 ●

　　在結婚紀念宴會 (wedding anniversary) 上致詞時,必須考慮到結婚年數和年齡這兩項重要因素。這類的紀念活動,通常都是祝賀對方的「長」和「老」。但在演說中却不可以使用 "long" 或 "old" 這兩個字。特別是在尊重「年輕」的歐美文化中,用 "old" 這個字給人一種前途暗淡的感覺,不合乎社交禮儀。因此,宜用 "enduring" (持久的) 這個字,來敘述「老」這件事實,較能給人溫馨關懷的感覺。

Unit 11
A Wedding Reception

● A Sample Speech ●

I would like to express our gratitude to you for inviting us to this wonderful wedding reception. Also, I would like to extend our warmest congratulations to the newlyweds, Mr. and Mrs. Brown.

I happen to know the groom quite well through our business dealings between his company and mine. I believe Mr. Brown is **by far** the most competent and efficient businessman I have ever met. Obviously his capabilities even outside of his profession have also been proved from the fact that he has married such a beautiful and intelligent bride.

Let me say, "congratulations" to you both, and Mr. Brown, I hope you will not work too hard and leave your wife alone too often.

ADVICE

參加外國友人或客戶的婚禮，免不了會用英文說幾句話。因為是較正式的場合，所以不宜太過戲謔。除了祝福的言語之外，可以把新郎或新娘的優點或趣事穿插其中，不過可別惡作劇。

結婚喜宴

● 演說實例 ●

　　你們邀請我們來參加這個美好的婚宴，我們非常感激。同時，我要向新人，布朗夫婦，致上我們最誠摯的祝賀。

　　我碰巧和新郎很熟，因為他的公司和我的公司有生意往來。我認為布朗先生是我到目前為止所認識，最能幹、最有效率的人。而且，我們從他娶到這麼美麗聰明的新娘看來，很顯然他還有超出專業以外的能力。

　　我要向你們兩位道賀，同時我希望布朗先生可不要工作過度，而常常冷落了嬌妻喔！

** gratitude〔'grætə,t(j)ud〕*n.* 感激　obviously〔'ɑbvɪəslɪ〕*adv.* 顯然的
reception〔rɪ'sɛpʃən〕*n.* 婚宴　newlyweds〔'njulɪ,wɛdz〕*n.pl.* 新婚夫婦
groom〔grum〕*n.* 新郎　competent〔'kɑmpətənt〕*adj.* 有能力的；能幹的
efficient〔ɪ'fɪʃənt〕*adj.* 有效率的　capability〔,kepə'bɪlətɪ〕*n.* 才幹

Useful Expressions

感謝受邀請

1. Thank you for inviting me to speak at this wonderful reception.

謝謝你們邀請我在這個美好的宴會上說話幾句話。

2. It is a great pleasure to be here to celebrate Mr. Jones' wedding.

能夠在這裏慶祝瓊斯先生大喜，真是一大榮幸。

3. I am very happy to join you in celebrating Mr. Brown's wedding.

我非常高興能和各位一起慶祝布朗先生的婚禮。

讚美新人用語

1. Mr. Jones is a hard-working businessman. I'm sure he'll go far.

瓊斯先生是位苦幹的企業家。我確信他一定會成功。

2. The bride is a *talented computer programmer*. The whole department admires her skill and creativity.

新娘是個才華洋溢的電腦程式設計師。全部門的人都很佩服她的技巧和創造力。

3. The two of you make a perfect couple.

你們真是天造地設的一對。

賀辭

1. The whole company *joins* me *in* wishing you a very happy married life.

公司全體同仁和我一起祝你們婚姻生活愉快。

** *go far* 成功；出名　　talented〔'tæləntɪd〕*adj.* 有才能的
programmer〔'progræmɚ〕*n.* 程式設計師
creativity〔krie'tɪvətɪ〕*n.* 創造力

2. Mr. Brown, with your youth and talent, I am sure that you will have a very happy married life.

布朗先生,以你的青年才幹,我相信你的婚姻生活將十分幸福美滿。

3. Congratulations and have a beautiful honeymoon.

恭喜你們,祝你們蜜月愉快。

● 演說小教室 ●

　　以下這篇是針對較熟識的外國友人或同事而寫的婚禮致詞;內容較不拘形式,以又羨慕又嫉妒的語氣給予新人祝福。

　　Hi, John and Jenny. I am really very happy for you two.

　　I've known John for some five years, and I have always been envious of his talent and abilities **in many respects.** He is not merely a competent professional in international trade; he is exceptional in doing almost anything. Today, I have become even more envious of John, because he just got married to one of the most beautiful brides in the world.

　　But don't let our envy bother you, John, because we want you to become the happiest couple in the world, and keep us **envious of** you two.

　　Congratulations, and be happy!

　　嗨!約翰、珍妮,我真為你倆感到高興。

　　我認識約翰已經五年了,我一直嫉妒他在各方面的才能,他不僅是一位能幹的國貿人才,而且在各方面也都很傑出。今天我更嫉妒約翰了,因為他剛娶了世界上最美麗的新娘之一。

　　不過,可別太介意,因為我們希望你們是世界上最幸福的一對;而且請讓我們繼續嫉妒下去吧!

　　恭喜你們,祝你們快樂!

**　envious〔ˈɛnvɪəs〕*adj.* 嫉妒的　respect〔rɪˈspɛkt〕*n.* 方面
professional〔prəˈfɛʃənḷ〕*n.* 專業人員　exceptional〔ɪkˈsɛpʃənḷ〕*adj.* 特別的

Unit 12
Receiving an Award

● A Sample Speech ●

Ladies and gentlemen, Mr. President, and all the distinguished guests. I can't believe that I have **been selected as** the Employee of the Year. When I was **informed of** my nomination, **I couldn't believe my ears.** In fact, I am still not sure if I really deserve this honor, because I know many of my colleagues work even harder than I do.

I want to take this opportunity to thank them all, and share with them the pleasure and honor of receiving this award. Thank you very much, and I'll try my best to **contribute to** the further growth of our company.

ADVICE

接受頒獎時的致詞，最重要的是「態度」問題。如何表現得恰到好處，謙虛有禮，以下四項原則可供參考：①正式的受獎致詞中，宜以 " Ladies and gentlemen, … " 這類問候語開始②坦率地說出得獎的心情③讚美或感謝同事、家人等的協助與鼓勵④對未來做個結論或期許。

接受頒獎

● 演說實例 ●

　　各位女士，各位先生，董事長，以及各位貴賓：我簡直無法相信我會當選為本年度的模範員工。當我得知被提名時，我自己也不敢相信。事實上，到現在為止，我還不能確認，自己是否真的應該獲得這項榮譽，因為我知道同事當中比我更努力的大有人在。

　　我要籍這個機會向他們道謝，並把獲獎的快樂與榮耀與他們分享。非常感謝各位，我一定會盡全力貢獻自己，使我們的公司更加成長。

** distinguished〔dɪ'stɪŋgwɪʃt〕*adj.* 顯著的；傑出的
inform〔ɪn'fɔrm〕*v.* 通知　　　　nomination〔nɑmə'neʃən〕*n.* 提名
deserve〔dɪ'zɝv〕*v.* 值得　　　　contribute〔kən'trɪbjut〕*v.* 貢獻

Useful Expressions

稱呼與問候

1. ***Ladies and gentlemen***, Mr. Chairman, and honorable judges.....

各位女士，各位先生，主席，以及各位可敬的評審們。

2. Mr. Chairman, members of the board....

主席，各位董事…。

3. Hello, everybody. (*informal*)

嗨，大家好！（非正式）

4. Good evening, everyone.

各位晚安！

表達獲獎的心情

1. I am very happy to receive this award.

能獲得這個獎，我很高興。

2. It is an honor and a privilege to receive this award.

能獲得這個獎，是一項榮譽，也是一種榮幸。

3. I am very happy that my work has received such recognition.

我的工作受到如此肯定，我非常高興。

獲獎時的謝辭

1. ***None of this would have been possible*** without the help and support of my friends.

如果不是朋友們的幫助及支持，這一切都是不可能的。

** honorable 〔'ɑnərəbl〕 *adj.* 可敬的   award 〔ə'wɔrd〕 *n.* 獎品
privilege 〔'prɪvɪlɪdʒ〕 *n.* 恩典；榮幸   recognition 〔rɛkəg'nɪʃən〕 *n.* 肯定
encouragement 〔ɪn'kɜɪdʒmənt〕 *n.* 鼓勵

2. I especially want to thank Mr. James for his continuous support and encouragement.

我特別要感謝詹姆士先生不斷的支持和鼓勵。

3. I want to thank all of you whose diligence and dedication *made this possible*.

我要感謝各位的勤奮工作及全心投入，才使我獲得這次榮譽。

4. I believe that they also deserve this award, and I think I *happen to* represent them in accepting this award.

我相信他們也應該獲獎，而我只是僥倖代表他們接受這項獎而已。

5. They have always been my precious team mates, advisers, and above all, friends.

他們一直是我最珍貴的工作伙伴、顧問及朋友。

** diligence 〔'dɪlədʒəns〕 *n.* 勤勉
dedication 〔dɛdə'keʃən〕 *n.* 奉獻
represent 〔,rɛprɪ'zɛnt〕 *v.* 代表

● 演說小教室 ●

　　我們常從電視上看到各類頒獎典禮的實況,得獎人(winner)的致詞方式真是五花八門，有的全副武裝，以西裝禮服上台，有的則標榜奇裝異服，甚至穿件破牛仔褲。有些則因驚訝過度而目瞪口呆，有的則意氣風發，說些:「我辦到了！」(I've done it!)之類的話。其實，在國際社交場合上，**端莊合宜**的態度還是受到肯定的，得獎人還是應該對觀眾率直地表示出喜悅之情，如 " I can't tell you how happy I am. " 並以 "Without the great help from my friends, none of this would have been possible " 這句話向朋友道謝，同時也顯現出你**謙沖為懷**的氣度。

Unit 13
Offering an Award

• A Sample Speech •

Good morning, everyone. I have asked you here this morning in order to recognize some of our employees for their outstanding performance in the past year.

Based on **careful consideration and performance evaluation,** the selection committee has reached the following decision: the three recipients of the Outstanding Performance Award are Mr. David Hsu... Ms. Jenny Lee... and Mr. John Wu.

Needless to say, this years recipients deserve special recognition for their dedication and accomplishments. Also, I would like to say that every one of you who wasn't chosen today has a good chance of winning this honor, if you try hard enough. I wish you all the best of luck.

ADVICE

主持頒獎典禮的致詞中，首先要明確地說出這次集會的目的。公佈獲獎人名單時，語氣要放慢一些，以製造每個人都有希望的氣氛。此外，不必指出是誰決定獲獎人選，最好用「由～委員會」決定來表示其公平性。在結束致詞之前，不要忘了鼓勵沒得獎的人。

主持頒獎典禮

● 演說實例 ●

　　大家早。今天早晨我請各位到這裏來，是為了要表揚過去一年來表現傑出的幾位員工。

　　在評估各位的表現，並經過審慎考慮之後，選拔委員會已經做成以下的決定：表現傑出獎的三位獲獎人是徐大衛先生、李珍妮小姐、以及吳約翰先生。

　　不用說，今年的受獎人，都是因為他們的貢獻和成就，而獲得特別的褒獎。但是我還想告訴今天沒有得獎的各位，如果你們努力嘗試，一定也有很好的機會可以獲得這項榮譽。我祝各位好運。

** recognize〔'rɛkəg,naɪz〕v. 表揚
outstanding〔aʊt'stændɪŋ〕adj. 傑出的
evaluation〔ɪ,væljʊ'eʃən〕n. 評估　committee〔kə'mɪtɪ〕n. 委員會
recipient〔rɪ'sɪpənt〕n. 接受者　dedication〔dɛdə'keʃən〕n. 奉獻
accomplishment〔ə'kɑmplɪʃmənt〕n. 成就

Useful Expressions

頒獎的致詞

1. I am pleased to announce the recipients of this year's Award for Outstanding Performance.

我很高興，能宣佈今年表現傑出獎的受獎人。

2. We are very happy to present the Award for Best Teamwork to the sales department.

我們非常高興，要把最佳團隊工作獎頒給銷售部。

3. We are gathered here to honor Mr. Walker's *dedication to* our company for the past thirty years.

我們今天齊聚一堂，是爲了表揚沃克先生過去三十年來來對我們公司的貢獻。

宣佈獲獎人名單

1. The three recipients of the Dedication Award are as follows :

三位貢獻獎的獲獎名單如下：

2. The winners of the Award for Excellence are...

獲得最佳表現獎的是…。

3. The *award committee* has reached a unanimous decision to give this award to Mr. Jackson.

頒獎委員會已經達成一致的決定，把這個獎頒給傑克森先生。

** announce〔ə'naʊns〕 *v.* 宣佈　　teamwork〔'tim'wɜk〕 *n.* 團隊合作
excellence〔'ɛkṣləns〕 *n.* 傑出
unanimous〔jʊ'nænəməs〕 *adj.* 全體一致的

4. Each recipient will be presented
   with a cash award of $20,000
   together with a certificate.

每位得獎人將獲得獎金二萬
元和一張獎狀。

5. Let us ***proceed to*** the presentation of awards by President Chang.

接下來請張董事長為我們頒
發獎品。

稱讚獲獎人

1. The three recipients deserve this a-
   ward for their dedication and ability.

這三位受獎人因為貢獻及能
力卓越,所以應該得獎。

2. Mr. White ***is*** well ***known for*** his
   creative work.

懷特先生的創造力是眾所周
知的。

3. I would like to acknowledge Mr.
   Goldberg's contribution by giving
   him this award.

我想把這個獎頒給古得伯格
先生,以表揚他的貢獻。

4. We are very proud of Ms. Jameson
   for her excellent performance.

我們替詹森小姐傑出的表現
感到很驕傲。

** certificate 〔sə'tɪfəkɪt〕 *n.* 獎狀;證書　　proceed 〔prə'sid〕 *v.* 進行(動作)
   acknowledge 〔ək'nɑlɪdʒ〕 *v.* 表揚;承認
   contribution 〔ˌkɑntrə'bjuʃən〕 *n.* 貢獻

● 演說小教室 ●

　　典禮進行成功與否,關鍵全掌握在**司儀**(Master of Ce-
remonies)的手中。司儀(M.C.)創造典禮氣氛的要訣不
外是①熟記與典禮進行有關的常用句。②利用「**停頓**」製造
緊張的氣氛。如在揭曉時說:" And the winner is…",在
is後停頓一下,是司儀慣用的技巧。③強調幽默感,蘊釀觀
眾和諧愉快的情緒。

Unit 14
Expressing Gratitude

● A Sample Speech ●

First of all, I want to thank you all for coming to this party.

Looking back, it seems like a very short five years living here and working together with you. The first few months were difficult, but I tried very hard to **adapt to** the new environment, new lifestyle, and new place of work.

There were times of disappointment and anger, and there were times of joy and excitement. Through them all, you have always been there to share them with me, and I **am** deeply **grateful to** you for that. Thank you all.

ADVICE

以上的致詞,是用在對朋友,同事表達謝意的宴會上,如從海外分公司要調回總公司的前夕、得獎後的慶功宴或私下聯誼請客等,尤其在外商公司,良好的人際關係是和工作能力成正比的。派駐海外的業務人員也不妨入境隨俗,從請客開始,打入外國友人的生活圈。

表達謝意

● 演說實例 ●

　　首先，我要感謝各位光臨這個宴會。

　　回顧以往，我住在這裏，跟各位一起工作的五年，似乎是很短暫的時光。開頭幾個月比較難，不過我努力試著來適應新環境，新生活方式，以及新工作地點。

　　我有失望、憤怒的時刻，也有喜悅、興奮的時刻。在這些不同的時刻中，各位總是在我身旁，和我一起分擔及分享，我深深感激你們！謝謝各位！

**　adapt〔ə'dæpt〕*v*. 適應　　environment〔ɪn'vaɪrənmənt〕*n*. 環境
disappointment〔,dɪsə'pɔɪntmənt〕*n*. 失望
grateful〔'gretfəl〕*adj*. 感激的

Useful Expressions

引起賓客注意的話

1. Does everybody have enough to eat? 　大家都夠吃嗎？

2. May I have your attention please?
   Jim has an announcement. 　請各位注意一下好嗎？吉姆有事情要宣佈。

3. *Gather around* — our host has
   something to say to us. 　請大家聚集過來——我們的主人有話要說。

表示感謝的話

1. I just want to thank you all for
   being such good friends. 　各位都是這麼好的朋友，令我感謝。

2. I don't know how to thank you
   for your kindness. 　你們對我這麼好，我不知要如何感謝。

3. I can't thank you enough for
   your thoughtfulness. 　你們這麼體貼，我怎麼感謝也不夠。

提及回憶

1. It's been a wonderful three
   years *working with you*. 　跟各位一起工作的三年，眞是美好的時光。

2. I will always remember the
   times I had here with you. 　我會永遠記得我跟各位在一起的時光。

3. The wonderful experience I have
   had here will remain in my memory forever. 　我將會永遠記得在這裏的一點一滴。

** host 〔host〕 *n.* 主人　thoughtfulness 〔'θɔtfəlnɪs〕 *n.* 體貼

● 演說小教室 ●

有時邀請外國客戶（business partner）來參加 thank-you party 也有助於增進雙方公司間的合作關係。如果能用英語致詞，則更能顯示出你的誠意。

We have asked you to come to our "Thank-you Party" today to show our gratitude to all of you for being our reliable business partners.

As you all know, doing business is not an easy thing. There may be different ways of doing business: some do it for an endless pursuit of profit, and others, for the well-being of society. One thing, however, that **we should not forget in doing business is to have a sense of appreciation.** A sense of regret or resentment will not help us in any way. Having a sense of appreciation for all the people will keep us going on in business.

That is why we have asked you to come tonight. We really appreciate your being our partners. And I hope you have a good time tonight.

今天邀請各位參加我們的宴會，是為了表示對各位忠實客戶的感激之意。

正如大家所知，做生意不是件容易的事。生意可以有許多不同的方式：有些人是為了追求無窮的利益，有些人則是為了社會的福祉。然而在經商時，我們不能忘的是要長懷感謝心。遺憾或憎恨無法幫助我們，唯有對所有人心懷感激，才能幫助我們長久經營。

這也就是今晚邀請各位光臨之因。我們非常感激各位做為我們的工作夥伴，同時希望今晚大家能玩得愉快。

** profit〔ˈprɑfɪt〕*n.* 利益　　appreciation〔ə͵priʃɪˈeʃən〕*n.* 感激
regret〔rɪˈɡrɛt〕*n.* 悔恨；遺憾　　resentment〔rɪˈzɛntmənt〕*n.* 憤恨

Unit 15
Self-introduction

● A Sample Speech ●

A Hello, it's a pleasure to meet you all. I am Sally Wang. I am from Taipei, Taiwan. This is my third trip to the United States, and I really **enjoy it**. I am working for a trading company as an assistant manager in the overseas distribution section. Thank you.

B I'm Philip Lui. I am a system engineer for IBM. My job is to develop new computer software, and I enjoy the job very much, because software development is very creative and imaginative work. So if anyone here is interested in computers and computer software, **please let me know**. We can spend hours talking about computers.

C Hello, everybody. I am George Lin from Taipei. I am working for an agent for an electric company. **It has been about five months since I** came to the United States, and I miss my family very much. It'll be several months before they come here, and I hope to continue to have an enjoyable single life till then. Thanks.

ADVICE

在社交場合做自我介紹時，要按照當時的氣氛或對象，來決定演講的內容，及要如何表現自己。以上是 3 個典型的例子 A 外交辭令型：主要是稱讚當地的種種，如「喜歡當地」等。B 工作中心型：以工作為重點，詳述工作的內容，不太談到自己的生活細節。C 個人接觸型：以生活細節為主，適合較輕鬆的場合。

自我介紹

● 演說實例 ●

A 嗨，很高興認識大家。我是王莎莉，我來自台灣台北。這是我第三次到美國，我很高興能留在這兒。我在一家貿易公司的國外行銷部門擔任協理的工作。謝謝！

B 我是菲利浦‧劉。我是 IBM公司的系統工程師。我的工作是發展新的電腦軟體，我很喜歡這份工作，因為軟體的發展是一種非常有創造力和想像力的工作。所以如果在座有人對電腦和電腦軟體感興趣，請讓我知道，我們可以用點時間來討論一下。

C 嗨，大家好。我是喬治‧林，來自台北。我目前在為一家電子公司的代理公司工作。來到美國已經五個月了，我很想念我的家人。他們會在幾個月後到美國來，我希望在那之前，我能繼續過我快樂的單身生活。謝謝。

** assistant〔əˋsɪstənt〕*adj.* 輔助的　assistant manager 協理
distribution〔͵dɪstrəˋbjuʃən〕*n.* 分佈；銷售
software〔ˋsɔft͵wɛr〕*n.* 軟體　agent〔ˋedʒənt〕*n.* 代理商

Useful Expressions

外交辭令型

1. It's a pleasure to speak to you. 　能跟各位說話是我的榮幸。

2. My name is Bob Young, and I work as a sales manager for an automobile company. 　我是鮑伯・楊，在一家汽車公司擔任銷售經理。

3. Chicago is a nicer place than I thought. 　芝加哥比我想像中好太多了。

工作中心型

1. Well, it's finally my turn to speak. 　嗯，終於輪到我了。

2. I've been working for CitiBank for about ten years, and now I am *in charge of* the foreign exchange section. 　我在花旗銀行已經工作了大約十年，現在我負責外滙部門。

自我中心型

1. Hello, it's really great to get to know each other. 　嗨，我們能彼此認識眞好。

2. My name is Sarah Wang, and I work for an *insurance company* in Tainan. 　我的名字是莎拉・王，我在台南的一家保險公司工作。

3. I was born and raised in Taipei, and my hobbies include tennis and yoga. 　我出生於台北，並在那裏長大。我的嗜好有是網球和瑜珈

4. If anyone here has one of these hobbies, let me know. 　如果在座各位和我有同好，讓我知道。

** in charge of 負責　　exchange〔ɪks'tʃendʒ〕*n.* 滙率
insurance〔ɪn'ʃʊrəns〕*n.* 保險　yoga〔'jogə〕*n.* 瑜珈

● 演說小教室 ●

　　在正式場合中很少需要做自我介紹,通常都有人會居間介紹,但萬一被指定做自我介紹時,必須注意是否「言之有物」。所以在平常就應該多準備一些自我介紹的「**關鍵字**」(＇key words),以此為中心來發言。以下 "harmony" 就是關鍵字,可以加深別人對自己的印象。

　　Ladies and gentlemen. Thank you for giving me an opportunity to speak about myself on this special occasion. I am Philip Lee, executive manager of the sales department of Delta Electric. In the three years since I have taken charge of the department, the sales of our products have grown astronomically and I am really proud of my department and staff. Some people sometimes ask me what is the secret of such tremendous growth, and I always answer : "Harmony in the department." Harmony in the department seems to have emerged as a result of mutual trust and respect between myself and my staff.

　　Well, it really was a great honor to speak to you, and I hope this gathering will help keep our harmony till the end. Thank you.

　　各位先生女士,謝謝大家給我機會,在這個特別的場合裏自我介紹。我是菲利浦‧李,台達電機銷售部的經理。在我接管銷售部的三年裏,我們的產品銷售量大爲增加,我以我們整個部門和員工們爲傲。有人問我如此驚人的成長率秘訣何在,而我總是回答「整個部門的和諧」。整個部門的和諧,則是由我自己和員工之間相互的信賴和尊重所產生的。

　　嗯!非常榮幸能跟大家說幾句話,希望這個聚會有助於我們維持圓滿和諧,謝謝!

** executive manager 經理　　astronomically〔ˌæstrəˈnɑmɪkl̩ɪ〕*adv.*龐大地 tremendous〔trɪˈmɛndəs〕*adj.* 巨大的　harmony〔ˈhɑrmənɪ〕*n.* 和諧 mutual〔ˈmjutʃʊəl〕*adj.* 相互的

Unit 16
Introducing Others

● A Sample Speech ●

Ladies and gentlemen, it is a great pleasure to have you all here this evening. Before we **start with** the lecture, may I say a few words about tonight's speaker?

Tonight's speaker, **as you all know**, is Mr. Hong Fu Man, currently president of Hong Trading Company. Mr. Hong was born in Shanghai, and grew up there until the war. He fled to Hong Kong, started his own business, and you know the rest of the story.

Forty years later, Mr. Hong is the owner of one of the leading companies in Hong Kong. Tonight he will speak to us on the topic, " Global Management in the 1990's." **Ladies and gentlemen, Mr. Hong Fu Man.**

ADVICE

在公司會議或國際會議中，都有機會公開引介重要人士出場。此時，在致詞時，首先向出席者道謝，在本論中，則簡單介紹演講者的經歷、背景。在結尾部分明確地指出演講的題目（ topic），最後則請演講者出場，結束這篇介紹辭。

引介他人

● 演說實例 ●

　　各位女士，各位先生：今天晚上各位能夠光臨，真是我們的一大榮幸。在演講開始以前，請容我介紹今晚的演講人。

　　各位都知道，今晚要為我們演講的，是目前洪氏貿易公司董事長，洪福滿先生。洪先生出生於上海，並在上海長大。戰爭爆發後，他逃到香港，並開創了自己的事業。接下來的故事，各位都很清楚。

　　四十年之後，洪先生成為香港一家首屈一指的公司的老板。今天晚上，他要為我們演講的主題是「一九九○年代的全球性經營」。各位女士、各位先生，洪福滿先生。

** lecture〔'lɛktʃɚ〕*n.* 演講　　currently〔'kɝəntlɪ〕*adv.* 目前
flee〔fli〕*v.* 逃跑（動詞三態為 flee, fled, fled）
global〔'globl̩〕*adj.* 全球的

Useful Expressions

介紹詞的開場白

1. It is a great pleasure to introduce the distinguished scholar, Mr. Anderson.

我很榮幸要為各位介紹著名的學者，安德生先生。

2. I would like to introduce tonight's speaker, Ms. Lisa Watkins.

請容我介紹今天晚上的演講人，莉莎，瓦特金斯女士。

3. Before we ask Ms. Feldstein to begin her speech, *let me say a few words by way of introduction.*

在我們請費爾茲坦女士演講之前，請先讓我做個簡短的介紹。

4. Tonight's speaker, Dr. Henry Jackson, needs no introduction.

今晚的演講人，亨利·傑克森博士，不需要我多做介紹。

5. Dr. Evans *is* internationally *renowned for* his best-selling book, "How to Live Healthfully."

伊凡博士以他的暢銷書"如何活得健康"而享譽全球。

介紹詞的主體

1. He was born in New York in 1940, and graduated from Harvard with an MBA. Then he went to work for IBM.

他於一九四〇年出生在紐約。他是哈佛大學的企管碩士，畢業之後，在 IBM 工作。

** distinguished 〔dɪ'stɪŋgwɪʃt〕 *adj.* 著名的；傑出的
graduate 〔'grædʒʊ,et〕 *v.* 畢業

2. He is a ***true-blue New Yorker***. He was born and raised in Brooklyn, and went to school at CUNY.

他是個道地的紐約人。他在布魯克林土生土長，並且上紐約市立大學。

3. He worked for the ABC company for thirty years until he started his own business.

他在 ABC 公司服務了 30 年之後，自行創業。

介紹詞的結尾

1. Let's have ***a big welcome for*** tonight's guest speaker, Mr. Frank Johnson!

讓我們熱烈歡迎今晚要演講的貴賓,法蘭克•強生先生。

2. Tonight he will speak about his thought-provoking best-seller, " The End of the World."

今天晚上，他將跟我們談他發人深思的暢銷書，「世界末日」。

3. Ladies and gentlemen, ***let me present Dr. John Smith.***

各位先生、各位女士，讓我我們歡迎約翰•史密斯博士。

** true-blue 〔'tru'blu〕 *adj.* 忠誠的；道地的
CUNY 紐約市立大學 (= *City University of New York*)
renowned 〔rɪ'naʊnd〕 *adj.* 著名的
thought-provoking 〔'θɔtprə,vokɪŋ〕 *adj.* 發人深思的
best-seller 〔'bɛst,sɛlə〕 *n.* 暢銷書

● 演說小教室 ●

　　根據研究指出，人類百分之七十的溝通，是透過「非語言」的方式來完成的。因此，如**臉部表情**(facial expressions)、**手勢**(gesture)、**姿勢**(posture)等**肢體語言**(body language)在演講、致詞時都扮演著重要角色。但要注意，肢體語言的使用和「文化」有密不可分的關係；不但不容易學，而且容易給人東施效顰的印象。因此唯有多看多聽，經常演練才能熟能生巧。

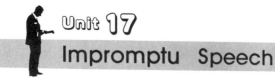

Unit 17
Impromptu Speech

● A Sample Speech ●

Well, I almost had a heart attack when they asked me to make a speech in English. I guess I didn't have one, though, since I'm still standing here.

Foreign languages have always been difficult for me. I took English, Spanish, and French in school, but I flunked all those classes. But since then, I have learned the most important language. It is the language of trust, openness, and understanding. This universal language has always brought people of different cultures together.

Thank you for giving me an opportunity to speak to you. And next time, please warn me in advance!

ADVICE

被邀請參加晚宴時，突然被要求用英語講幾句話，任何人都會措手不及的。但聽衆不會要求臨時被抓出來的人，要講得很出色。他們比較注意的是演講者的「反應」。因此當別人要求你演講時，大可不必隱藏自己慌亂的心情，乾脆承認自己會緊張，以及不擅長英語等話題，這也是一種演說技巧的運用。

即席演說

● 演說實例 ●

　　嗯，當他們要我用英文演講時，我差點就心臟病發作。不過，還好沒有發作，因為我現在還站在這裏。

　　外國語言對我來說一直很困難。我在學校裏修過英文、西班牙文和法文，可是全都當掉了。不過，從那時起，我學了一種最重要的語言，也就是信任、寬大以及互相理解的語言。這種世界通用的語言總是能夠使不同文化的人團結在一起。

　　謝謝各位給我這個說話的機會。此外，如果下次還有這種狀況，請預先告訴我。

**　heart attack　心臟病　　flunk〔flʌŋk〕*v.* 考試不及格
openness〔'opənnɪs〕*n.* 公開；率直　universal〔junə'vɝsḷ〕*adj.* 普通的

Useful Expressions

即席演講的開場白

1. Well, I didn't really expect to **make a speech** today.

   嗯，我實在沒有料到今天要演講。

2. If I had known that I would be speaking tonight...

   假如我早知道今晚要演講的話…

3. I'm a little nervous about making a speech in English, but I'll **try my best.**

   用英文演講，我有點緊張，不過我會盡力。

4. They say that misfortune comes when you least expect it. Well, I can tell you — it's true.

   人們說，不幸總在你最沒有料到的時候降臨——我可以告訴各位,這是千眞萬確的。

謙稱英語不好

1. Most Chinese **have trouble making speeches**, especially in English. Well, I am no exception.

   大部分中國人對於演講都有困難，特別是用英語演講。嗯，我也不例外。

2. I was born and raised in Taiwan. I'll try my best, but don't expect Shakespeare.

   我是台灣土生土長的。我會盡全力，但是請各位不要期待會聽到莎士比亞般的英文。

** nervous 〔'nɜvəs〕 *adj.* 不安的   misfortune 〔mɪs'fɔrtʃən〕 *n.* 不幸
exception 〔ɪk'sɛpʃən〕 *n.* 例外
Shakespeare 〔'ʃek,spɪr〕 *n.* 莎士比亞（英國大文豪）

3. I should mention that in school I flunked English *from time to time*. I hope I'll get at least a B today.

我要告訴各位，我在學校的時候，英文常常被當。希望今天我至少能得個B。

結尾

1. I want to thank you for asking me to speak tonight.

感謝大家今晚讓我講話。

2. Thank you for giving me an opportunity to speak to you.

謝謝各位能給我說話的機會。

3. I've really enjoyed speaking to you tonight.

今晚能跟各位演講，我感到非常愉快。

** *from time to time* 時常

● 演說小教室 ●

沒有事先準備，突然進行的演講，稱為 Impromptu Speech（**即席演講**）。演講時，除了要「準備內容」外，「心理準備」也是不可缺少的因素。即席演講與普通的 Prepared Speech 最大的不同點在於聽眾的「期待度（expectations）」。

當你突然被叫上台時，聽眾決不會像聽有準備的演講一樣，要求你也按照起承轉合的原則來說話。他們所要求的是，緩和情緒的「**一帖清涼劑**」，所以，演講時心情放輕鬆一點，即使講得不好也無所謂，而且最重要的是輕薄短小，就是所謂的" Take it easy, and be brief."。

Unit 18
Opening a New Branch

● **A Sample Speech** ●

Ladies and gentlemen, first of all I would like to thank you for coming to celebrate the opening of our new branch office.

This branch is the 25th office we have established **so far**. I am very happy that we have finally opened a branch in this area. **Taking all of the circumstances into consideration**, I believe the future of our company greatly **depends on** whether we will be able to do business here.

In order to successfully operate our branch, we need the support of customers like yourselves. We will do the best we can to serve you. Thank you very much.

ADVICE

分公司（branch office）開幕的致詞，主要是針對當地的客戶而做。在開頭中先向出席者致謝，在本論中則提及新設分公司的功能及重要性。結論必須抓住客戶的心，拜託他們支持，以維護分公司的順利營運。

開幕典禮致詞

● 演說實例 ●

　　各位女士，各位先生：首先，感謝各位前來，慶祝我們新設分公司開幕。

　　這間分公司是到目前為止，我們所設立的第二十五家。我們終於在這個地區設立了分公司，我感到非常高興。把所有狀況都列入考慮之後，我相信我們公司的未來，將大大仰賴於我們是否能在此地拓展業務。

　　我們需要像各位這樣的客戶支持，我們的分公司才能夠順利地營運。我們將會盡全力來為各位服務，謝謝！

＊＊ branch office 分公司　　　***take ～ into consideration***　　將～列入考慮
circumstance〔'sɝkəm,stæns〕*n.* 情況
successfully〔sək'sɛsfəlɪ〕*adv.* 順利地；成功地

Useful Expressions

開幕詞的開場白

1. Thank you all for coming to celebrate the opening of our new office.

感謝各位能夠前來，慶祝我們新的辦事處開張。

2. Thank you for *taking the time* to join us.

謝謝各位抽空前來。

3. I highly appreciate your presence here.

非常感激各位的光臨。

提到新設分公司

1. This new branch will play an important role in attracting new customers.

在吸收新客戶方面，這家新的分公司將扮演重要的角色。

2. Having a branch here in New York means a great deal to us.

在紐約設立分公司，對我們來說意義非凡。

3. To have a new branch here allow us to have a *worldwide distribution network* to supply our products all over the world.

在此地的新設分公司，使我們的產品可藉由全球性的行銷網遍銷全世界。

** appreciate 〔ə'prɪʃɪ,et〕 *v.* 感激　　attract 〔ə'trækt〕 *v.* 吸引
network 〔'nɛt,wɜk〕 *n.* 網路

結尾

1. We are looking forward to doing business with you.

我們期待和各位有業務往來。

2. I appreciate your support and understanding.

感謝各位的支持及諒解。

● 演說小教室 ●

外國客戶舉行分公司開幕酒會，而你被邀請致詞時，講稿最好**短一點**，並且要記得祝賀新設分公司前途光明。

Congratulations on the completion and opening of the new Taipei branch! I am very excited to see this luxurious office, and happy to know that the Bank of America has opened another branch in Taiwan. As the relationship between the R.O.C. and the United States strengthens more and more, having this new branch means a great deal to the economy of both countries.

I hope you will be able to do a good business with the Chinese as well as with customers of other countries, and good luck to this wonderful new branch.

首先恭賀這家新的台北分公司順利完工及開幕！看到這麼舒適豪華的辦公室，真是令人興奮。知道美國銀行又在台灣開了另一家分公司真是令人高興。由於中華民國與美國的關係目益加強，相信這家分公司對兩國的經濟有重大的意義。

我希望你們能和中國人有良好的商業關係，就如同和其他國家的顧客一般。最後，祝福這家新的分公司有美好的前途。

** ***do business with*** *sb.* 和某人做生意
luxurious 〔lʌg'ʃʊrɪəs〕 *adj.* 豪華的
completion 〔kəm'pliʃən〕 *n.* 圓滿
economy 〔ɪ'kɑnəmɪ〕 *n.* 經濟

Unit 19
Celebrating a Success

● A Sample Speech ●

After two months of negotiations, our company has finally won our first major contract with the EC. For us, this event represents the start of a new era.

At this time I would like to take this opportunity to thank our staff for all they have done to make this occasion possible. Many of you have **worked overtime** to keep this project **on schedule**. For those of you who have sacrificed your evenings and weekends, the company owes you a great deal. **Needless to say,** your efforts will be remembered when promotion time comes.

It is our hope that this contract will represent the beginning of a long and fruitful cooperation between our company and the EC, as well as between the company and our staff. Thank you, and enjoy the party!

ADVICE

公司舉辦慶功宴時，上司主管不免會上台說幾句話。這時若有外國人在場，你不妨用英文來致詞，增加新鮮感。首先將要慶祝的事由陳述一遍，最重要的是感謝員工的努力，當然別忘了論功行賞。結尾則以對未來的期許作結束。

慶功宴

● 演說實例 ●

　　經過二個月的交涉，我們公司終於贏得了與歐洲共同體第一項主要合約。對我們來說，這件事代表著一個新紀元的開始。

　　此刻，我想藉著這個機會謝謝全體員工，都是你們的努力，我們才有今天的慶功宴可開。各位當中有許多人，都必須加班，才能使這項計畫趕上進度，對於那些犧牲夜晚及週末的同仁，公司十分感激你們。不用說，升遷時刻到來的時候，公司一定會記得你們的辛勞。

　　我們希望，這項合約不僅代表著本公司及全體員工之間，也代表著本公司與歐洲共同體之間，長久而有利的合作關係。謝謝各位，請盡情地玩！

** negotiation 〔nɪ͵goʃɪˋeʃən〕 *n.* 交涉；談判　　era 〔ˋɪrə〕 *n.* 時代
EC 歐洲共同體（ European Community ）
contract 〔ˋkɑntrækt〕 *n.* 合約　　***work overtime*** 加班
sacrifice 〔ˋsækrə͵faɪs〕 *v.* 犧牲　 owe 〔o〕 *v.* 欠
promotion 〔prəˋmoʃən〕 *n.* 升遷　 cooperation 〔ko͵ɑpəˋreʃən〕 *n.* 合作

Useful Expressions

▎慶祝的事項

1. Our two companies have finally reached an agreement.

我們兩家公司終於已經達成協議。

2. At last we have obtained government approval.

我們終於得到政府的同意。

3. In the end our joint venture will prove a success.

我們共同的冒險最後一定會成功。

▎象徵意義

1. This agreement represents five months of negotiations.

這項協議是交涉了五個月的成果。

2. This event *stands for* a new era in the history of our company.

在我們公司的歷史上，這件事代表著新紀元的開始。

3. The contract *symbolizes our fruitful cooperation*.

這項合約象徵著我們之間有利的合作。

4. This agreement sums up a 20-year working relationship.

這項協議概括說明了二十年的工作關係。

5. This project is an example of our company's dynamism.

這項計畫顯示出本公司的活力。

** obtain 〔əb'ten〕 *v.* 獲得 approval 〔ə'pruvḷ〕 *n.* 贊成；同意
joint 〔dʒɔɪnt〕 *n.* 聯合 venture 〔'vɛntʃɚ〕 *n.* 冒險
symbolize 〔'sɪmbḷ͵aɪz〕 *v.* 象徵 *sum up* 概括；總結
dynamism 〔'daɪnə͵mɪzəm〕 *n.* 活力

感謝員工

1. This project was made possible by the efforts of our staff.

由於員工們的努力，這項計畫才得以完成。

2. Government subsidies enable us to compete effectively.

政府的資助使我們眞正具備了競爭力。

3. I don't know what we would have done without Mr. Wang.

如果沒有王先生的話，眞不知道我們怎麼辦。

4. We couldn't have done it without Ms. Lee.

如果沒有李小姐，我們就無法完成這件事。

5. We *owe* it all *to* the support of our employees.

所有一切，都歸功於全體職員的支持。

** subsidy 〔'sʌbsədɪ〕 *n.* 補助金；資助
effectively 〔ɪ'fɛktɪvlɪ〕 *adv.* 有效地

compete 〔kəm'pit〕 *v.* 競爭

● 演說小教室 ●

　　不管是演講或談生意時，我們不想說的事，往往用 " I don't know" 這句話來敷衍過去。然而，在這句話之後必須要有 " follow-up "。如果在 " I don't know "後面不講任何話，不只會暴露出自己的無知，也會讓人誤會你沒有在聽他說話。

　　如果對自己的回答沒有把握時，可以先用 " As far as I know "（就我所知）或 " If I remember correctly "（如果我沒記錯的話）這種條件句，再敘述自己的見解。這樣就不會因為中斷，而出現冷場的情況。總之，應該絕對避免只說 " I don't know " 而沒有下文的情形。

Unit 20
The Company Anniversary Party

● A Sample Speech ●

Ten years ago today, Mr. Hsu rented a small apartment not far from here, which some of the older employees may remember. Pretty soon he had hired a few of his classmates, and then they were hiring people, too. Now there are over a thousand of us.

Our products are sold in over sixty different countries. Of course, **the bottom line is... well, the bottom line,** and our company netted over eighty million dollars last year. We all have reason to be very proud.

In ten years, Mr. Hsu has brought us from a one-room business to the fifth-largest peripherals manufacturer in Taiwan. I'm confident that we will see even greater success in the decades to come.

ADVICE

公司的週年慶（Anniversary Party）上，常會邀請外國客戶一起共襄盛舉。這時，嘗試用英語來致詞，不僅可讓員工們興緻高昂，又可表示出對外國友人的尊重。演講中所提的公司草創經過及業績成長情形，亦有助於公司形象的建立。

公司週年慶

● 演說實例 ●

　　十年前，徐先生在離這裏不遠的地方租了一間公寓，比較資深的員工可能還記得。很快地，他聘用了一些他的同班同學；然後這些人又再雇用其他的人。如今，我們已經有了一千名員工。

　　我們的產品銷售六十幾個不同的國家。當然囉，重點還是在我們的盈虧，而去年我們公司淨賺八千萬元以上。我們都有理由感到很驕傲。

　　在十年當中，徐先生把我們從一個房間的公司，提昇到全台灣第五大周邊設備製造商。我確信，在未來的歲月裏，我們將會看見更大的成就。

** net〔nɛt〕*v.* 淨賺　　***bottom line***　重點；盈虧（指損益表最末行）
peripheral〔pəˈrɪfərəl〕*n.* 周邊產品；周邊設備
manufacturer〔ˌmænjəˈfæktʃərə〕*n.* 製造業者
confident〔ˈkɑnfədənt〕*adj.* 確信的　　decade〔ˈdɛked〕*n.* 十年

Useful Expressions

驕傲

1. We have reason to be very proud.

我們很有理由可以驕傲。

2. We can all **take pride in** our company's accomplishments.

我們可以以公司的成就自豪。

3. I am very proud of our success.

我對我們的成功感到很驕傲。

敘述歷史

1. Ten years ago, our company was founded.

我們公司創立於十年前。

2. **Pretty soon**, our company expanded.

不久，我們公司就擴大了。

3. Then we moved to our new headquarters.

然後，我們遷到新的總部去。

4. Now we are one of the largest companies in Taiwan.

現在，我們是台灣最大的公司之一。

5. We have gone from a small company to one of the industry giants.

我們已經從小公司變成企業界的巨人。

** accomplishment 〔əˈkɑmplɪʃmənt〕 *n.* 成就　　found 〔faʊnd〕 *v.* 創立
expand 〔ɪkˈspænd〕 *v.* 擴大　　headquarters 〔ˈhɛdˈkwɔrtəz〕 *n. pl.* 總部
giant 〔ˈdʒaɪənt〕 *n.* 巨人

展望未來

1. The future is bright for our company.

我們公司的前途一片光明。

2. I'm sure we will remain strong *for many years to come.*

我確信,在未來的日子裏,我們公司都將保持強勢。

3. We can look forward to exciting growth *in the years ahead.*

我們可以期待,在未來的歲月裏,會有驚人的成長。

● 演說小教室 ●

　　說話的速度,也是演講時的重要因素。有時為了製造出沈靜的氣氛,也必須把話說慢一點。一張打字用紙的演講稿差不多可以說**兩分鐘**左右。所以,當你必須做五分鐘的演講時,應該準備三張打字用紙的演講稿。但有一點必須注意,如果用同一種速度把演講稿,從頭到尾唸一遍,聽眾一定會覺得單調無趣。為了避免這個毛病,可以根據內容改變一下說話的速度,一般來講,**重要的地方慢慢講**,其他部分則可以快一點。

數字英語①

在進行演說時，常用到數字。如果平常不習慣用英語講數字，一旦上台就緊張講不出來。

★ 整數

1000 以上的數目，從後面算起，每三位數爲一個單位來唸。

398	three hundred and ninety-eight
2,457	two thousand four hundred and fifty-seven
6,381,911	six million three hundred eighty-one thousand nine hundred and eleven
10 億	one billion（美），one thousand million（英）
100 億	ten billion（美），ten thousand million（英）
1,000 億	one hundred billion（美） one hundred thousand million（英）
1 兆	one trillion（美），one billion（英）

★ 小數

小數點讀做 point，小數點以後的數字則一個一個唸。0 讀做 naught 或 zero。

1.35	one point three five
25.402	twenty-five point four zero two
0.34	point three four

Chapter
3

業務簡報演說
Informative
Speeches

Unit 1

Introducing the New Boss

● A Sample Speech ●

Ladies and gentlemen, it is a great pleasure to have you all here to welcome our new company president, Ms. Windy Chou.

I would like to give you a brief profile of Ms. Chou for those of you who do not know her well. Ms. Chou **graduated from** Fu Jen University in 1960. Right after graduation she started working for our company in the sales department. After ten years overseas, she returned to become executive manager of the sales department, where she has remained until now.

Ladies and gentlemen, our new president, Ms. Windy Chou !

ADVICE

在正式會議中介紹新任上司之前，必須事先收集被介紹者的個人經歷、背景等相關資料。介紹時可分為兩方面來說，一是有關優秀工作能力方面的職位與表現，二是關於個人方面，如強調對方平易近人的個性，及休閒嗜好。

介紹新任上司

● 演說實例 ●

　　各位女士，各位先生：很高興，各位能夠共同歡迎我們公司的新任總經理，周溫蒂女士。

　　因為各位當中有部份對周女士不太熟悉，所以就讓我做一個簡單的介紹。周女士一九六〇年畢業於輔仁大學。她一畢業，就開始在本公司的銷售部門工作。之後，她出國十年。歸國後，她便擔任銷售部執行經理迄今。

　　各位女士，各位先生，我們的新任總經理，周溫蒂女士！

** president〔'prɛzədənt〕*n.* 總經理　　profile〔'profaɪl〕*n.* 簡要描述

　　　　executive〔ɪg'zɛkjʊkɪv〕*adj.* 執行的　　manager〔'mænɪdʒə〕*n.* 經理

Useful Expressions

介紹新上司的開場白

1. May I introduce you to our new manager, Mr. Peters?

請讓我介紹我們的新任經理，彼得斯先生。

2. For those of you who have not met him, let me give a short personal history of our new vice president.

因為有些人還沒有見過我們的新任副總經理，所以就讓我簡單介紹一下他的個人經歷。

3. Allow me to introduce our new company advisor, Mr. Samuel James.

請容我介紹我們公司的新任顧問，山米爾‧詹姆士先生。

介紹新上司的工作狀況

1. He has accomplished a great deal over the past twenty years.

在過去二十年中，他成就非凡。

2. His *contributions to* our company have been so enormous that he deserves this new position.

他對我們公司貢獻如此卓越，與新職位實至名歸。

3. His experience and insight will be invaluable.

他的經驗及洞察力是非常珍貴的。

4. His exceptional talent and ability will doubtlessly *contribute to* further development of our company.

以他卓越的才能，定對公司更進一步的發展貢獻良多。

** advisor〔əd'vaɪzə〕*n.* 顧問 　accomplish〔ə'kɑmplɪʃ〕*v.* 完成；實現
contribution〔,kɑntrə'bjuʃən〕*n.* 貢獻
enormous〔ɪ'nɔrməs〕*adj.* 巨大的 　insight〔'ɪn,saɪt〕*n.* 洞察力

介紹上司的嗜好及個性

1. He is *not only* a competitive businessman, *but also* a music lover and a chess enthusiast.

他不僅是一位具有競爭力的企業家，同時也熱愛音樂及下棋。

2. There is a warm, caring side to this aggressive person.

他是個積極進取的人，但是也有溫和、親切的一面。

3. He is very aggressive in business, but *at the same time*, a good husband and a caring father of three Children.

他不僅在事業上積極進取，同時在家庭中，他也是一位標準丈夫和三個小孩的慈祥爸爸。

4. He never wastes time even while he *is away from* work.

甚至在不工作的時候，他也不浪費一分一秒。

5. You will be surprised to know that he *played the go-between* for more than twenty *happily married couples* for the past fifteen years.

要是你們知道，過去十五年來，他已經撮合了超過二十對以上的佳偶，一定會非常驚訝。

** competitive 〔kəmˈpɛtətɪv〕*adj.* 具有競爭力的
enthusiast 〔ɪnˈθjuzɪˌæst〕*n.* 熱心家　caring 〔ˈkɛrɪŋ〕*adj.* 關懷的；親切的
aggressive 〔əˈgrɛsɪv〕*adj.* 積極進取的
the go-between 媒人（＝matchmaker）

● 演說小教室 ●

　　在使用**肢體語言**（ body language ）方面，有時光靠多看多聽可能效果也有限。而且勉強地做手勢、露出假笑，常會發生反效果。因此最重要的是保持**自然**的態度，基於自己本身的經驗，再加上運用聽眾可接受的肢體語言。

　　此外，很多人說話時，有凝視著天花板的習慣，這會給人**不誠實**的印象。因此，演講時最好儘量目視聽眾。

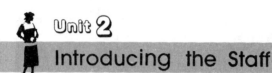

Unit 2
Introducing the Staff

● A Sample Speech ●

We are very happy that you have come **all the way** to Taipei to visit our company. We may be small, but we **think of** our company **as** one big happy family.

Let me introduce you to our staff. Sitting in the center of our office is Mr. Lee, the head of our department. He is our boss, but he never **bosses** us **around**. Across from Mr. Lee's desk are Mr. Kao, Mrs. Wu, Mr. Liu, and Mrs. Lui.

So that is our department. We hope you will enjoy visiting with us.

ADVICE

有一天,幾位外國客戶來訪, 來到你所管轄的部門視察,如果你能簡短地介紹你部門的特徵及員工 , 必能加深彼此之間的情誼。以上的演說辭 , 可能對你有幫助 。

介紹部門職員

● 演說實例 ●

　　各位大老遠來到台北參觀我們的公司，我們感到非常高興。我們公司是小了一點，可是我們都把它當成一個快樂的大家庭。

　　讓我向各位介紹我們的同仁。坐在辦公室中間的，是我們這個部門的主管，李先生。雖然他是我們的上司，可是他却從不隨意指使我們。坐在李先生對面的是高先生，吳太太、劉先生以及劉小姐。

　　這就是我們這個部門的成員。我們希望各位的參觀愉快。

** staff〔stæf;stɑf〕*n.* 全體同事
boss** *sb.* **around 指使某人

Useful Expressions

介紹公司或部門特徵

1. Our company **takes into** special **consideration** the needs of our workers.

我們公司特別關切員工的需要。

2. There are many unique, creative personalities in our department.

我們這個部門裏，有許多旣獨特，又具創造力的人才。

3. Our department **takes pride in** having close ties among the staff, just like a family.

我們部門以如一家人般的和諧關係爲傲。

員工介紹

1. Sitting at the head of the table is our department manager, Mr. Herbert Fox. We all think he **looks like** Robert Redford.

上座的是我們這個部門的經理，赫伯特・福克斯先生。我們都覺得他很像勞勃・瑞福。

2. Mr. Jenkins has the respect of the entire staff for his patience and thoughtfulness.

詹肯斯先生有耐性，又很體貼別人，所以受到全體員工的尊敬。

** consideration〔kən‚sɪdə'reʃən〕*n*. 考慮；體恤
unique〔ju'nik〕*adj.* 獨特的　personality〔‚pɝsn̩'ælətɪ〕*n*. 人物
patience〔'peʃəns〕*n*. 耐性　　thoughtfulness〔'θɔtfəlnɪs〕*n*. 體貼

▌結尾

1. I hope this will give you a good idea of who's who in our department.

   希望這個介紹讓各位知道了我們這個部門裏誰是誰。

2. If there is anyone who has not been introduced, please let me know.

   如果還有人沒被介紹到，請告訴我。

3. If anyone has something they would like to say, *please go ahead*.

   如果任何人有話要說，就請直說。

4. I think I have introduced everyone.

   我想每個人都介紹過了。

5. I believe that concludes the introduction of our staff.

   我想就介紹到這裏。

   ** conclude〔kən'klud〕 v. 終結

● 演說小教室 ●

　　替外國客戶介紹公司職員時，密訣在點出各部門的**特色**，如強調像一家人（family）般的和諧氣氛，或擁有獨特（unique）的創意人才等。介紹在場的人時，表示**位置**的說法也很重要，如 sit at the center（坐在中間）、across from（對面）、from right to left（從右到左）等。

Unit 3
About Recreational Facilities

● **A Sample Speech** ●

Our company has a great deal to offer **in the way of** social opportunities. We have more than thirty activity groups organized by workers for athletic and recreational purposes.

Among those groups are the Tennis Club, Aerobics Club, and Basketball Club. And for those of you who want to **slim down**, our Aerobics Club welcomes anybody, male or female, who wants to have a good workout.

Please take advantage of these group activities and enjoy yourself.

ADVICE

在為外國客戶簡介公司的簡報會議上，或為新進員工舉辦的迎新會中，可用英語來談談公司內部的休閒活動，讓他們在聽完有關工作方面的介紹之後，調劑一番。如果公司的團康活動很多，則只需要做幾個簡單的介紹即可。結尾別忘了呼籲他們擁躍參加這些社團。

簡介團康活動

● 演說實例 ●

　　我們公司提供許多的社交機會。我們員工所組成的運動及休閒團體超過三十個。

　　這些團體中包括網球社、有氧舞蹈社、籃球社等。至於想要身材苗條的人，不論男女，我們的有氧舞蹈社都歡迎你們去好好鍛鍊一下。

　　請多多利用這些社團活動，盡情地玩。

**　athletic〔æθ'lɛtɪk〕*adj.* 運動的
　　recreational〔,rɛkrɪ'eʃənḷ〕*adj.* 休閒的；消遣的
　　aerobics〔ɛ'robɪks〕*n. pl.* 有氧健身法；有氧舞蹈
　　slim〔slɪm〕*v.* 減輕體重　　work-out〔'wɜk,aʊt〕*n.* 鍛鍊身體

Useful Expressions

▌ 介紹社團的開場白

1. Our company offers **a variety of** recreational opportunities.

我們公司提供各種不同種類的休閒機會。

2. We make a special effort to make your life comfortable and enjoyable.

我們特別盡力,來使各位的生活舒適愉快。

3. We encourage our employees to organize groups for recreational and entertainment purposes.

我們鼓勵員工,組織休閒性及娛樂性的團體。

4. I believe the employer should serve employees not only by giving salaries, but also by providing opportunities for them to enjoy their lives.

我認爲公司不僅要以薪水的方式照顧員工,而且還要提供他們享受生活樂趣的機會。

▌ 社團的數目及目的

1. We have **as many as** twenty groups which you are welcome to join.

我們的社團多達二十個,歡迎各位加入。

2. There are fifteen company-funded group activities, **with an average of** 30 members each.

由公司資助的團體活動有十五項,平均每項有三十人參加。

** employee 〔͵ɛmplɔɪˈi;ɪmˈplɔɪ‧i〕 *n.* 員工　encourage 〔ɪnˈkɝɪdʒ〕 *v.* 鼓勵
entertainment 〔͵ɛntəˈtenmənt〕 *n.* 娛樂　fund 〔fʌnd〕 *v.* 籌備基金

3. These activities will give you an opportunity to meet people from other departments.

這些活動提供一個機會，讓各位可以見見其他部門的員工。

呼籲參加社團

1. You *are not obligated to* participate, but I can guarantee that if you do you will have a good time.

並不強迫參加，但是我保證參加之後會很愉快。

2. If you would like to know more about any of these groups, please ask your colleagues for further information.

如果各位對任何社團還想有更進一步的認識，請向同事們詢問，他們會提供較深入的資訊。

3. Please *feel free to* join one of these company-owned recreational groups.

請儘量踴躍參加這些由公司提供的團康活動。

** provide〔prə'vaɪd〕v. 提供　obligate〔'ɑblə,get〕v. 強迫
participate〔pɑr'tɪsə,pet〕v. 參與　guarantee〔,gærən'ti〕v. 保證
colleague〔'kɑlig〕n. 同事

● 演說小教室 ●

　何謂有效利用空間的演說？所謂空間（Space），指的是進行演講的場地範圍、演說者站的地方，和聽眾之間的距離。講演者最理想的位置，是站在最容易吸引聽眾注意的地方。譬如會議室中，主席通常坐在上座，因為那是最容易吸引與會人員注意的位置。

　相反的，如果主席坐在會議桌的正中央，會議的進行狀況會如何呢？與會人員會精神不集中，會議的進展也會很緩慢。所以，自己站在最容易吸引聽眾注意的地方，不只能夠讓聽眾專心聽演講，也有提高演講者的權威和可信度的效果。

Unit 4
Introducing the Company

● A Sample Speech ●

It is a great pleasure to have you visit us today. I am very happy to have the opportunity to introduce our company to you.

Our company was established in 1950 by Mr. Kuanming Yeh. We **specialize in** manufacturing electronic goods and exporting them all over the world. We grossed about US $100 million last year, and our business is growing steadily. Our offices are in Asia, North America, and Europe, with about 1000 employees, and we're working diligently to serve the needs of our customers.

In order to further develop our overseas market, we need reliable agents to market our products. I hope you will seriously consider **doing business with us.** Thank you.

ADVICE.

因拓展業務或因應外國客戶考察而必須用英語做公司簡介時，可參考以上的範例。在介紹公司時，有關公司的統計數字千萬不可以說錯，如創辦年份，員工人數，年度營業額等，都必須給人明確的數字概念，客戶才容易具體地了解公司的營運狀況。

公司簡介

● 演說實例 ●

　　各位今天來參觀本公司，是我們極大的榮幸。我能有這個機會來向各位介紹本公司，心中感到非常愉快。

　　本公司是葉寬明先生于一九五○年創設的。我們專門製造電子產品，並外銷世界各地。去年我們的總營業額大約為一億美元，而我們的業務還在穩定地成長之中。我們的分公司遍佈亞洲、北美洲以及歐洲；我們的員工約有一千人，大家都勤奮工作，以滿足顧客的需求。

　　為了更進一步拓展我們的海外市場，我們需要可靠的代理商來銷售我們的產品。我希望各位能夠認真考慮和我們進行生意往來，謝謝！

**　** establish 〔ə'stæblɪʃ〕 v. 建立　　specialize 〔'spɛʃəl,aɪz〕 v. 專門化；專精
manufacture 〔,mænjə'fæktʃə〕 v. 製造
electronic 〔ɪ,lɛk'trɑnɪk〕 adj. 電子的　　gross 〔gros〕 v. 總獲利
diligently 〔'dɪlədʒəntlɪ〕 adv. 勤奮地　　reliable 〔rɪ'laɪəbl̩〕 adj. 可靠的
agent 〔'edʒənt〕 n. 代理商

Useful Expressions

介紹公司的開場白

1. I would like to introduce our company to you.

   我來向各位介紹本公司。

2. Let me *talk a bit about* our company.

   讓我簡單地談一談本公司。

3. May I say a few words about our company?

   我可以介紹一下本公司嗎？

4. I hope you can get a picture of what our business is from my introduction.

   希望經由我的介紹，各位能對本公司的業務有個初步的了解。

公司的營運狀況

1. We specialize in importing foreign-made products and marketing them across the nation.

   我們專門進口國外的產品，並在國內銷售。

2. We have been exporting autombiles for many years, and *enjoy a good reputation* among our customers.

   我們從事汽車外銷已經許多年，我們的顧客都給予我們很好的口碑。

3. We *deal with* a lot of foreign companies, and are considered to be one of their most reliable agents.

   我們跟許多外國公司有生意往來，而他們都認為我們是最可靠的代理商之一。

** import〔ɪm'port;ɪm'port〕 *v.* 進口；輸入
export〔ɪks'port;'ɛksport〕 *v.* 出口；外銷
reputation〔,rɛpjə'teʃən〕 *n.* 名譽；名聲

公司的統計資料

1. Our company was founded in 1890 and is one of the oldest and most reliable in the country.

本公司創立於一八九〇年，而且是全國最悠久、最可靠的公司之一。

2. We have six branches nationwide, ***with more than 1000 employees.***

我們在全國有六家分公司，員工超過一千人。

3. Our company grosses about US $160 million, and business is growing rapidly.

我們公司的總營業額大約爲一億六千萬美元，而我們的業務正在快速成長當中。

4. The annual business gross of our company during the past decade has averaged about US$160 million.

近十年來，本公司的年度平均獲利淨額是一億六千萬美元。

** branch〔bræntʃ〕*n.* 分部；分公司
nationwide〔'neʃən,waɪd〕*adj.* 遍及全國的　annual〔'ænjuəl〕*adj.* 每年的
gross〔gros〕*n.* 總計；總數　average〔'ævərɪdʒ〕*v.* 平均

● 演說小教室 ●

　　演講時的**姿勢**（posture）也會帶給聽衆各種不同的印象，有給人舉止非凡的印象，也有給人軟弱無力的感覺。這和個人的個性、以及平時是否留心有關。一般而言，最便於做演講的姿勢，稱爲「**放鬆的姿勢**」。就是把心情放輕鬆，不要使身體太僵硬。人一緊張，不只身體生硬、動作不靈活，連舌頭也會不聽使喚。

　　這裏有個秘訣可以幫助你放鬆身體，就是把**雙脚張開與肩膀同寬**，使整個身體站穩。另外也有一些緩和緊張的方法，譬如將**一隻手輕輕地放在口袋裏，把手放在桌沿**，或**握住麥克風**。

Unit 5
Introducing the Enterprise

● A Sample Speech ●

Let me briefly discuss how our company works.

Our company **consists of** three major divisions: management offices, a research institute, and manufacturing plants.

First, we have ten management offices throughout the world. The main office **is located** here in Taipei.

Second, we have a very innovative research institute where about 300 scientists are developing new products.

Third, we have three manufacturing plants which operate on a sophisticated computer system.

I have given you a **bird's-eye view** of our company, and now I would like to **entertain your questions**.

ADVICE

有人問起公司各個組織的實際狀況、營運方式時，可參考以上的演講稿，開頭先說明要談的主題，其次分為三個重點，最後則針對這三點做詳細的說明，在以傳遞訊息（ information）為主的演講中，需要這種明白通暢的結構。

企業簡介

● 演說實例 ●

讓我簡短地說明本公司營運的方式。

本公司由三個主要的部份所組成：管理部門、研究部門以及工廠。

首先，我們在全世界有十個管理處，總部就設在台北。

其次，我們有一個研究中心，非常具有創新性；裏面大約有三百名科學家在從事新產品的開發。

第三，我們有三間工廠，完全依照先端的電腦系統來運轉。

這就是我們公司的概況。現在，我來回答各位的問題。

** consist 〔kən'sɪst〕 v. 包括；由～組成　　division 〔də'vɪʒən〕 n. 部分；部門
institute 〔'ɪnstə,tjut〕 n. 研究所；協會　　locate 〔lo'ket〕 v. 設於
innovative 〔'ɪnə,vetɪv〕 adj. 革新的；創新的
sophisticated 〔sə'fɪstɪ,ketɪd〕 adj. 複雜的；先端的
bird's-eye 〔'bɝdz,aɪ〕 adj. 鳥瞰；概觀的
entertain 〔,ɛntə'ten〕 v. 娛樂；使滿意

Useful Expressions

介紹公司組織的開場白

1. Let me describe how our company is organized.

讓我來介紹一下本公司的組織。

2. I am going to briefly outline our company's organization.

我要概略地說明本公司的組織。

3. I would like to **touch upon** how our company is organized.

我來提一提本公司的組織。

公司的組織

1. Our company **is composed of** three offices and five factories.

本公司是由三個辦事處以及五間工廠所構成的。

2. We have a main office in Taipei and many overseas agents.

我們的總公司在台北,並有許多國外的代理商。

3. **In addition to** our main office, we have twenty branch offices across the nation.

除了總公司之外,我們在全國還有二十家分公司。

4. In each branch we have about fifty employees **on average**.

平均每間分公司有五十名員工。

** describe〔dɪ'skraɪb〕v. 描述;介紹　organize〔'ɔrgən,aɪz〕v. 組織
outline〔'aʊt,laɪn〕v. 敍述要點　**touch upon** 提及
compose〔kəm'poz〕v. 構成　factory〔'fæktrɪ;'fæktərɪ〕n. 工廠
agent〔'edʒənt〕n. 代理商　**in addition to** ～ 除了～之外
on average 平均

組織各部份的職責

1. Each of the five plants maintains a high productivity with their so-phisticated manufacturing facilities.

這五家工廠都必須以它們高水準的製造設備，來維持高度的生產力。

2. The main office *is responsible for* marketing and distribution.

總公司負責產品的行銷及分配。

3. Offices in other locations act *according to* the directions of the main office.

其他地方的辦事處則根據總公司的指導運作。

4. The main office *specializes in* personnel management, planning, advertising and selling.

總公司專門負責人事管理、企劃、廣告及銷售業務。

** productivity〔͵prodʌk'tɪvətɪ〕*n.* 生產力
facility〔fə'sɪlətɪ〕*n.* 設備
distribution〔͵dɪstrə'bjuʃən〕*n.* 分配；流通

● 演說小教室 ●

　　演講時的**表情**，會給聽眾留下很大的印象。臉部表情可以很清楚地表現出緊張、疲勞、喜悅、焦慮等情緒，這不是本人的意志所能控制的。不管演講的內容多麼精采，一旦露出沒有信心、膽怯的神情，這場演說還是欠缺說服力的。

　　控制表情的方法，首先是「**不要低頭**」。頭一低下來，不但給人膽怯的感覺，而且也由於**眼神**沒有和聽眾接觸，而無法吸引他們的注意。另外一個方法是「**慢慢地說**」，慢慢說話可以使心情穩定，臉部表情自然就輕鬆起來，態度也會顯得從容不迫。

Unit 6
Exhibiting New Products

● A Sample Speech ●

Today I have the great pleasure of announcing our new portable **video camera** called "Take it Easy." Let me tell you about some of the features of this new product.

First, compared to other video cameras that are already available on the market, Take it Easy is very light **in weight.** It weighs only 2 pounds, so you can carry it **without difficulty.** In fact, you can film with one hand without ever getting tired.

Second, the price will be about half that of other video cameras. Thus, Take it Easy is sure to satisfy the needs of the consumer.

ADVICE

這類演講的重點，在強調新產品的優點。因此，有效的演講步驟，就如範例所示，將新產品的優點，用第一（first）、第二（second）的形式分條說出來。最後在結論中再用一句話，做概括性的評論。

新產品發表會

● 演說實例 ●

　　今天，我非常榮幸，要來介紹我們最新型的手提錄影機，「輕鬆拍」。請讓我向各位說明這種新產品的特點。

　　第一，跟其他已經上市的攝影機比起來，「輕鬆拍」是非常輕巧的一種機型。它只有兩磅重，所以各位要攜帶，絕對沒有困難。事實上，各位還可以用單手拍，而不會感覺到累。

　　第二，「輕鬆拍」的價格將是其他攝影機的一半。因此，「輕鬆拍」一定會滿足顧客的需求。

** announce〔ə'naʊns〕*v.* 發表　　portable〔'pɔrtəbḷ〕*adj.* 手提的
video camera 錄影機　　feature〔'fitʃɚ〕*n.* 特色
available〔ə'veləbḷ〕*adj.* 可用的；有效的
film〔fɪlm〕*v.* 拍攝　*n.* 影片　satisfy〔'sætɪsfaɪ〕*v.* 滿足

Useful Expressions

介紹新產品的開場白

1. I am very happy to announce our new AX-1 model computer.

我非常高興能發表我們最新的電腦機型「AX-1」。

2. Let me introduce Hi-Fi A, our new video recorder.

讓我向各位介紹「Hi-Fi A」(「高傳眞A」),我們最新型的錄影機。

3. I would like to announce a new word-processor called "X-Act".

我現在要介紹一種新型文字處理機,「X-Act」(「X行動」)。

新產品的特徵

1. Our new personal computer has many features.

我們的新型個人電腦擁有多項特色。

2. Among its many features is an efficient, powerful memory.

它的許多特徵之一,就是效率高、威力強大的記憶裝置。

3. Our new *video recorder* is better, cheaper, and more durable than any other on the market.

我們的新型錄影機,比市面上任何機種的品質好,價格低,而且更耐用。

4. *First*, it gives better colors and sounds.

首先,它擁有較好的色彩和音質。

5. *Second*, it has better durability. It can last a life-time.

其次,它耐用性高,可用一輩子。

** processor〔ˈprɑsɛsə〕*n.* 處理;裝置　efficient〔əˈfɪʃənt〕*adj.* 有效率的
video recorder 錄影機　durable〔ˈdjʊrəbl〕*adj.* 耐用的

6. ***Third,*** the price is the lowest of all the video recorders.

第三，它的價格是所有錄影機中最低的。

結論

1. I am sure that this new model will ***be well-received*** by our customers.

我相信這種新機型一定會受到顧客的歡迎。

2. I am sure that Hi-Fi A will compete well in the market.

我確信「Hi-Fi A」具有強大的市場競爭力(銷路一定會很好)。

3. I am sure that our customers will welcome its innovative features.

我確信新產品創新的特點，一定會受到顧客歡迎。

4. I hope my brief explanation will help you to realize the great potential of this product.

希望我簡短的說明能夠幫助各位瞭解這項產品雄厚的潛力。

** compete〔kəmˈpit〕*v.* 競爭　　potential〔pəˈtenʃəl〕*n.* 潛力

● 演說小教室 ●

　　在眾人面前說話，常會因為大家的眼光都看著你，而令你緊張得說不下去。此外，也不是每位聽眾都用友善的眼神注視你，所以更會讓你覺得侷促不安。尤其是走向麥克風、站到眾人面前的那一刻，聽眾投過來的視線，甚至讓你想臨陣脫逃。此時，你千萬不可因此而不看聽眾的眼睛，故意避開他們的視線。

　　而對付「視線的壓力」的秘訣，就是一邊**尋找對你充滿善意的眼神**，一邊說話，而不要去管其他冷淡的眼光。然後，把自己的視線投注在**猛點頭**的人那邊，如此就可以讓你充滿信心地講下去。

Unit 7

Sales Talk

● A Sample Speech ●

Let me describe our new product and then show you how it is better than those of any other manufacturers.

First, our Super XYZ, with its excellent memory capacity and processing ability, performs better than any other word-processor on the market today.

Second, the Super XYZ **comes equipped with** a highly-efficient electronic printer that can print 500 words per second. Furthermore, Super XYZ allows for the use of up to six different languages.

Third, with its retail price of US$250, Super XYZ offers the lowest price ever in the word-processor market.

Thus, I have no doubt that our new word-processor Super XYZ has all the features that are required of a successful product.

ADVICE

首先在開頭中以破題的方式,點出演說的目的:「我們公司的產品性能優越」。其次敘述爲何優越的理由(亦即指出優秀產品中,不可欠缺的特質)。最後再敘述三到五個特質,就是一篇條理分明的演講。在敘述新產品的「優點」時,也必須明確地說明此商品另一個魅力,亦即賣不賣得出去的問題。最好把此商品對消費市場的吸引力,做更詳細的說明。請記得演講稿中的三個步驟①目的,②理由,③個別的事實就可以了。

推銷產品

● 演說實例 ●

　　讓我向你們說明一下我們的新產品，並將其優於其它廠商的優點向你們展示。

　　第一，我們的「超級 XYZ」有最佳的記憶容量和處理能力，比目前市面上的任何其他文字處理機都要優良。

　　第二，「超級 XYZ」配備有高效率的電子印表機，每秒可印五百個字。此外，「超級 XYZ」還可以使用六種不同的語言。

　　第三，「超級 XYZ」以每台零售價二百五十元美金，提供了文字處理機市場，有史以來，最便宜的價格。

　　因此，我確信我們的新型文字處理機「超級 XYZ」，具備了一項成功的產品所需要的一切特質。

** capacity 〔kə'pæsətɪ〕 *n.* 容量　　perform 〔pə'fɔrm〕 *v.* 執行；表現
　retail price 零售價　　require 〔rɪ'kwaɪr〕 *v.* 需要

Useful Expressions

破題式的開場白

1. Let me show you how it **differs from** other products.

讓我來告訴各位，它和其他產品不同的地方

2. Let me show you some of the new features.

讓我來告訴各位（這項產品的）一些新特點。

3. I am going to explain briefly what makes our product different.

我來簡短地解說一下我們產品的不同之處。

4. Let me explain why our product will have a great appeal.

讓我來說明，我們產品為什麼具有那麼大的吸引力。

5. I want to talk about **the great potential of this product**.

我想來談談這項產品雄厚的潛力。

產品的優點

1. Our product's high quality guarantees excellent performance.

我們的產品品質一流，保證性能優良。

2. Our latest design will never fail to attract customers' attention.

我們最新的設計絕對能夠吸引顧客的注意。

3. Our new computer has all the earmarks of a **big seller**.

我們的新電腦具有暢銷品的一切特徵。

** appeal 〔ə'pil〕 *n.* 吸引力　potential 〔pə'tɛnʃəl〕 *n.* 潛力
guarantee 〔͵gærən'ti〕 *v.* 保證　attract 〔ə'trækt〕 *v.* 吸引
earmark 〔'ɪr͵mɑrk〕 *n.* 特徵

4. Our new word processor has everything you need at a price you can afford.

各位所需要的功能，我們的新型文字處理機都有，而且價格各位一定付得起。

結論

1. *In closing*, I would like to emphasize our high rate of customer satisfaction.

最後，我要強調，我們的產品一定能夠使顧客感到非常滿意。

2. Thus, I predict that our new video camera will be the best-selling camera in the years ahead.

因此，我預測在未來，我們的新型攝影機將會成為銷路最好的攝影機。

3. I hope my rough description has given you a better idea of our product.

希望我概略的說明使各位對我們的產品有了較深的認識。

4. I hope my brief presentation will help you understand our product's appeal.

希望我簡短的報告能夠幫助各位了解我們產品的吸引力。

** emphasize〔'ɛmfə‚saɪz〕*v*. 強調　predict〔prɪ'dɪkt〕*v*. 預測
best-selling〔'bɛst'sɛlɪŋ〕*adj*. 暢銷的

● 演說小教室 ●

　　做為一個成功的推銷員（sales），在向客戶介紹新產品之前，必須先做以下三項功課：① **愛自己的產品**：了解產品的優、缺點及開發這項產品的背景及思想。②**收集新資訊**：掌握各項與商品有關的情報，如客戶的價值觀、生活方式、產業動態、新的政令等。③**訓練完善的說明能力**：以模擬的方式，訓練自己可以從商品的任何一點講起。

Unit 8
The Yearly Routine

● A Sample Speech ●

Let me tell you about some of the annual events organized by our company.

The new **fiscal year** begins in July, when the **newly recruited employees** fresh from college join the staff. For these newcomers we give a welcome party in the second week of July. Also, we have a company excursion in the third week of September.

Toward the end of the year, we have a big year-end party to celebrate the passing of the year. On the second Sunday of March we have an intramural sports meet in which teams from each department participate. The fiscal year **concludes** in June **with** the annual stockholders' meeting.

ADVICE

介紹公司時,也經常會提到公司整年的例行活動(yearly routine)。這是表明公司提供員工福利的好機會,所以,如果只說明各活動的日期和場所,就失去介紹的意義。最好能將每個活動的目的及對員工的好處說出來,以吸引聽眾的注意。

例行活動簡報

● 演說實例 ●

讓我來告訴各位本公司的年度活動。

　　新的會計年度從七月開始，這時剛從大學畢業的新進人員會加入我們的行列。我們在七月的第二個星期，會為這些新進人員辦迎新。此外，在九月的第三週，我們將舉辦一次團體郊遊。

　　到了年底，我們會辦一個盛大的尾牙，來慶祝一年過去。在三月的第二個星期天，我們還有一項公司運動會，每個部門都要組隊參加。到了六月，年度股東會議開完之後，這個會計年度也就結束了。

** annual〔ˈænjʊəl〕*adj.* 一年的　　　fiscal〔ˈfɪsk!〕*adj.* 會計的
recruited〔rɪˈkrutɪd〕*adj.* 新招募的；新進的
excursion〔ɪksˈkɝʒən, -ʃən〕*n.* 遠足；郊遊
intramural〔ˌɪntrəˈmjʊrəl〕*adj.* 內部的
participate〔pɑrˈtɪsəˌpet, pəˈtɪsəˌpet〕*v.* 參與
stockholder〔ˈstɑkˌholdɚ〕*n.* 股東

Useful Expressions

介紹開場白

1. We organize *a variety of* events in which you can participate.　我們會舉辦各式各樣的例行活動，你們都可以參加。

2. We have various events for your relaxation and enjoyment.　爲了讓各位身心鬆弛、精神愉快,我們有許多的例行活動。

3. We offer a lot of activities to enrich your life.　我們提供許多活動，使各位生活更加豐富。

公司的例行活動

1. There is *a series of* training sessions designed for new employees.　我們爲新進人員設計了一連串的訓練課程。

2. We have an intensive English program for businessmen who plan to work overseas.　對於計畫到國外從事貿易工作的員工，我們有密集的英語課程。

3. We need volunteers to organize the *field day*.　我們需要自願者來籌畫戶外運動日。

4. We *wind up* the first half of the year *with* an overnight trip to Kenting.　我們以到墾丁的二天一夜旅行，作爲上半年度的結束。

** relaxation〔͵rilæks'eʃən〕*n.* 鬆弛　　enrich〔ɪn'rɪtʃ〕*v.* 使豐富
session〔'sɛʃən〕*n.* 課程　　intensive〔ɪn'tɛnsɪv〕*adj.* 密集的
volunteer〔͵valən'tɪr〕*n.* 自願者　　*field day* 戶外運動日

5. The field day is, of course, open to all the employees' families, relatives and friends.

當然，戶外運動日開放給所有員工的家人及親友參加。

6. Our employees *take turns in* going on company-paid assignments abroad every year.

我們的員工可輪流參加每年由公司資助的國外研習營。

7. For those superior employees, there will be a one week paid vacation leave in July.

資深員工在七月，有一星期由公司資助的旅遊假。

** superior 〔sə'pɪnɚ, su-〕 *adj.* 資深的；高級的
assignment 〔ə'saɪnmənt〕 *n.* 工作；任務

● 演說小教室 ●

Public Relations Department 公關部

General Affairs Department 總務部

Personnel Department 人事部

Accounting Department 會計部

Sales Department 業務部

Product Development Department 產品開發部

Chairman of the Board 董事長

President 〔'prɛzədənt〕 *n.* 總經理；總裁

Vice-President 〔,vaɪs'prɛzədənt〕 *n.* 副總經理

Director 〔də'rɛktɚ, daɪ'rɛktɚ〕 *n.* 主任；理事

Executive Manager 經理（部門主管）

Section Manager 課長

Assistant Manager 協理

Manager 〔'mænɪdʒɚ〕 *n.* 主任；管理者

Unit 9
Introducing Personnel Policy

● A Sample Speech ●

I would like to explain our company's personnel policy including promotion, transfer, retirement **and so on.**

With a few exceptions, we announce promotions and transfers on April 1 every year. The decision about promotions is based upon the judgment of the head of the department as well as the recommendations of the personnel committee. As to transfers, they are usually determined **on the basis of** the recommendations of the head of the department concerned. We have a flexible policy concerning transfers. That is, if an individual does not wish a transfer, she or he can decline the transfer appointment. As to our retirement policy, we set the retirement age at 60, and allow for earlier retirement if one wishes.

We endeavor to give all our employees **equal and fair treatment in** these matters. If you want to have more information, please contact the Personnel Department. Thank you.

ADVICE

員工最關心的事，莫過於昇遷（promotion）、調職（transfer）、退休（retirement）等有關人事方面的問題。因此在開頭中，即舉出將敍述的項目，在本論中則按照順序逐項說明。結尾則點出公司是以公平（equality）爲宗旨來處理人事問題，並樂意提供有關於人事方面的解答。讓員工感覺到公司方面的誠意。

人事制度簡介

● 演說實例 ●

　我要說明一下我們公司的人事度，包括昇遷，調職，退休等事宜。

　除了一些例外，我們會在每年的四月一日宣布昇遷和調職的消息。昇遷的決定是根據各部門主管的判斷和人事委員會的推薦；至於調職，則通常由相關部門主管的推薦來決定。關於調職，我們有一項彈性政策，也就是說，如果一位員工不希望調職，他（她）可以拒絕調職的任命。至於我們的退休制度，我們規定退休的年齡是60歲，而如果員工在60歲以前想退休，我們也會批准。

　在這些方面，我們努力給所有的員工公平的待遇。如果各位還想知道更多資訊，請和人事部聯絡。謝謝！

** transfer〔'trænsfɚ〕*n.* 調職　exception〔ɪk'sɛpʃən〕*n.* 例外
recommendation〔,rɛkəmɛn'deʃən〕*n.* 推薦
determine〔dɪ'tɝmɪn〕*v.* 決定　flexible〔'flɛksəbḷ〕*adj.* 有彈性的
concerning〔kən'sɝnɪŋ〕*prep.* 關於　decline〔dɪ'klaɪn〕*v.* 拒絕
endeavor〔ɪnd'dɛvɚ〕*v.* 努力　contact〔'kɑntækt〕*v.* 接觸；聯絡

Useful Expressions

發表的開場白

1. I am going to briefly describe
   how decisions about promotions,
   transfers and so on are made
   in our company.

   我將簡單地介紹一下，公司是如何決定昇遷、調職等事項。

2. Let me explain the process of
   decision-making *in regard to* promotions, transfers, and other matters.

   讓我說明一下關於昇遷、調職及其他事項的決策過程。

3. Let me illustrate our policy
   concerning promotion, transfer,
   wage hikes, and so on.

   讓我說明一下有關我們昇遷、調職和加薪等項目的制度。

關於昇遷、調職的說明

1. Promotions are decided by the
   recommendations from the company's advisory committee.

   昇遷的決定是根據公司顧問委員會的推薦。

2. We have a policy of transferring
   our personnel at least once during
   the first ten years of employment.

   我們有一項政策：員工在職的前十年內，至少調職一次。

** process〔ˈprɑsɛs, ˈprɔsɛs〕*n.* 過程　　*in regard to* 關於
　　illustrate〔ˈɪləstret, ɪˈlʌstret〕*v.* 舉例說明
　　hike〔haɪk〕*n.* 增加；提高
　　advisory〔ədˈvaɪzərɪ〕*adj.* 顧問的；諮詢的

結論

1. Our basic policy about personnel matters is equality and fairness. We are *making a great effort* to give everybody an equal opportunity.

我們對人事制度的基本政策是平等和公正。我們盡力給每一個人公平的機會。

2. What I have described *so far* is our basic policy.

到目前為止，我所敍述的就是我們的基本政策。

3. We are flexible enough to accommodate exceptions and negotiations.

我們有足夠的彈性接受例外的事件和磋商。

4. So please let us know whenever you *come across* some trouble in promotions and transfers. We will do the best we can to help you.

所以無論何時各位在昇遷和調職上遭遇問題，請讓我們知道。我們將會盡力幫助各位。

5. If you have comments, opinions, or criticism about our policy, please feel free to send them to the Personnel Department.

如果各位對於我們的制度有意見或批評，請不要客氣並告訴人事部。

** equality〔ɪ'kwɑlətɪ〕*n.* 平等　accommodate〔ə'kɑmə,det〕*v.* 接受；容納
negotiation〔nɪ,goʃɪ'eʃən〕*n.* 磋商；談判　criticism〔'krɪtə,sɪzəm〕*n.* 批評

───●演說小教室●───

在發表**新產品**、或**企劃**會議上演說時，可以利用**視聽器材**（audiovisual equipment）來輔助。如複合投影機（overhead projector），幻燈機、錄放影機等。此外，還可以用**圖表、照片**來增加整個演講的效果，使聽眾更容易瞭解。

使用這類機器時，要注意這不過是自己演講的「輔助」工具。絕不可本末倒置。在給聽眾看圖表的前後，必須將其內容做簡短的說明，以便他們能集中「注意力」在機器或銀幕上，來印證你的演說。

Unit 10
Production & Distribution

● A Sample Speech ●

Our company **takes pride in** its special production and distribution systems. Let me describe them briefly.

Our fully-automated factories **are equipped with** dozens of computer-controlled robots for high-precision manufacturing. The robots are accurate, efficient, and require little maintenance.

Our distribution system also **makes** effective **use of** computers. We have established an **on-line** communication system with dealers across the country in order to serve our customers **in the best way we can**.

ADVICE

在為客戶或新進人員介紹產銷程序時，必須注意儘量少用專業術語。Informative Speech 主要的目的就是用淺顯易懂的說詞，把「事實」傳達給對方。所以，即使你的專長是生產及運銷，也不須在此賣弄專業知識。

產銷程序報告

● 演說實例 ●

　　對於本公司獨特的生產及運銷體系，我們感到很自豪。讓我簡短地說明一下。

　　我們全自動化的工廠配備有數十個由電腦控制的機器人，從事高精密度的製造生產。機器人既準確又有效率，而且不太需要維修。

　　我們的運銷系統也有效地利用了電腦。為了要盡全力來服務顧客，我們也已經在全國的經銷商之間，建立了電腦連線的通訊系統。

**　distribution〔͵dɪstrə'bjuʃən〕*n*. 運銷　automate〔'ɔtə͵met〕*v*.自動化
　robot〔'robət〕*n*. 機器人　precision〔prɪ'sɪʒən〕*n*. 精確的
　accurate〔'ækjərɪt〕*adj*. 準確的　maintenance〔'mentənəns〕*n*.維修；保養

Useful Expressions

介紹產銷的開場白

1. Let me discuss our company's production and distribution system.

讓我來說明本公司的生產及運銷系統。

2. I would like to **comment on** how our products are manufactured and how they are distributed throughout the country.

我來解說一下我們產品的製造方式，及運銷過程。

3. Let me describe the production and distribution process.

讓我來描述一下生產及運銷程序。

公司產銷的特徵

1. We boast one of the largest distribution networks in the country.

我們以擁有全國最大的運銷網路之一而自豪。

2. Our production system **is characterized by** its efficiency.

我們生產系統的特點是效率高。

3. Our nationwide distribution network can supply **retail stores** directly from the factory.

我們遍佈全國的運銷網路，可以從工廠直接供貨給零售店。

** comment〔'kɑmɛnt〕*v.* 解說；註釋　boast〔bost〕*v.* 自誇
network〔'nɛt,wɝk〕*n.* 網路
characterize〔'kærɪktə,raɪz〕*v.* 以～爲特點
retail〔rɪ'tel〕*adj.* 零售的

結論

1. As you can see, our production process is very sophisticated.

就如各位所見，我們的生產程序極其複雜。

2. I have briefly ***touched upon*** the distribution process of our company.

以上我簡短介紹了本公司的運銷程序。

3. I have given you a rather simplified explanation of our production and distribution systems.

我相當簡單地為各位解說了我們的生產及運銷體系。

4. They are ***too*** complex ***to*** explain sufficiently in a short speech like this.

它們太複雜了，以致於無法在如此短的演說中作足夠的解說。

5. Please contact us at the ***Public Relations Department*** if you want to know more details.

如果各位想知道更多的細節，請與我們的公關部聯絡。

＊＊ simplified〔ˈsɪmpləˌfaɪd〕*adj.* 簡化的　　explanation〔ˌɛkspləˈneʃən〕*n.* 解說
complex〔ˈkɑmplɛks; kəmˈplɛks〕*adj.* 複雜的　　detail〔ˈditel; dɪˈtel〕*n.* 細節

● 演說小教室 ●

　　聲音（voice）和**腔調**（diction）是天生的，不可能一朝一夕就變好！但音質和措詞會影響整個演說，却是無可否認的事實。
　　根據某項研究指出：**聲音低沈**的男人比聲音尖銳的男人，較容易得到聽者的信賴。這可能是因為低沈的聲音，給人一種威嚴和沈著的感覺。但音色的好壞並無法自行控制，最重要的，還是必須把自己的聲音，**清清楚楚**地傳到對方的耳中。就算音色不甚理想，只要擁有自己的主張和信念，照樣可以聚集聽眾熱切的眼光。

Unit 11
The Corporate Philosophy

● A Sample Speech ●

Today I would like to briefly introduce you to our company's **corporate philosophy**. Since the founding of the company in 1955, we have **stood for** honesty and cooperation.

Honesty is the best way to win the trust of our customers. Cooperation is the best way to win their business. In order to compete **on an equal basis with** other companies, we make a special effort to establish good communication and cooperative relationships between management and labor so we can discuss any problems without hesitation.

Based on this philosophy, we hope to **contribute to** our customers, employees, and society **as a whole**.

ADVICE

這類的演說，一般的形式就像本篇的範例一樣，選出有關經營哲學的二、三個重點，然後依序敘述其重要性。各點的重要性可以用具體的例子來說明，讓聽衆比較容易瞭解。如：trust — good interpersonal relationship; honesty—win trust from customers; cooperation— competition with other companies.

公司經營哲學

● 演說實例 ●

　　今天，我想簡單地向各位介紹本公司的經營哲學。本公司自從一九五五年創立以來，就一直以誠實與合作為宗旨。

　　誠實是贏得顧客信賴的最佳方法，而合作則是贏得顧客生意的最佳方法。為了要和其他公司在公平的基礎上競爭，我們特別致力於在管理及員工之間建立良好的溝通管道以及合作關係，以便能夠毫不遲疑地討論各種問題。

　　基於這種哲學，我們希望對於我們的顧客、員工乃至於整個社會，都能夠有所貢獻。

** corporate 〔ˈkɔrpənt;ˈkɔrprɪt〕 *adj*. 企業的；團體的
philosophy 〔fəˈlɑsəfɪ〕 *n*. 哲學　　***stand for*** 以～為宗旨；贊成
cooperation 〔ko,ɑpəˈreʃən〕 *n*. 合作
hesitation 〔,hɛzəˈteʃən〕 *n*. 遲疑　　***as a whole*** 就整體而論

Useful Expressions

經營哲學的內容

1. Our *business philosophy* includes dedication and friendliness.

我們的經營哲學包括奉獻及友愛。

2. Our *management philosophy* suggests there should be cooperation with labor.

我們的經營哲學是，要與勞方建立合作關係。

3. Our business philosophy is reflected in our employees' dedication.

我們公司的哲學反映在員工的努力奉獻上面。

經營哲學的重點

1. It is important to trust your employees.

信任自己的員工是很重要的。

2. Cooperation is *as* important *as* competition.

合作跟競爭一樣重要。

3. We try to let our workers *compete with* one another, while maintaining a cooperative relationship among them.

我們讓員工們彼此競爭;同時也保持合作的關係。

4. Having trust in each other is very important because *doing business* requires good interpersonal relationships.

彼此之間的信任非常重要，因爲經營企業時需要良好的人際關係。

** competition〔,kɑmpə'tɪʃən〕*n.* 競爭
interpersonal〔,ɪntə'pɝsən̩〕*adj.* 人與人之間的

5. Being honest in business is indeed one of the best strategies in order to win trust from our customers.

經營時的誠實,的確是贏得顧客信賴最好的策略之一。

▌結論

1. I am very happy to have shared some of my personal views about management with you.

我很高興能夠和各位分享我個人的一些經營理念。

2. I have briefly outlined our business philosophy.

以上我簡短地概敍了我們的經營哲學。

3. I hope what I've said will be of help to you.

希望我剛剛所說將會對各位有所幫助。

4. If there are any questions, I'd be happy to answer them *on behalf of* the President.

如果有任何問題,我很樂意代表總經理來回答。

** strategy〔'strætədʒɪ〕*n.* 策略　　*on behalf of* 代表

● 演說小教室 ●

所謂**比喻**(metaphor)就是用具體的東西為例,來說明抽象的事物。若能巧妙地使用比喻,不但聽眾容易瞭解,而且能讓他們留下非常深刻的印象。如 "He's a ball of fire." 和 "He is energetic" 的意思相同。但 " a ball of fire " 比單純的 " energetic ",更能產生具體的想像,而留下深刻的印象。另外,把 " a ball of fire " 中的 " ball " 提出來,說成 "keep the ball rolling." 就變成「加油!」的意思。把 " fire " 提出來,說成 "Don't get yourself burnt out" 就變成「不要太勉強自己。」的意思。像這類語言遊戲,是歐美人特別喜歡的。

Unit 12
Market Research

● A Sample Speech ●

After extensive **market testing,** we have high expectations for our new Sugar Boomers breakfast cereal.

First, the results from the shopping simulation test: Fot this test we recreated the shelves of a typical supermarket, stocked them with breakfast cereals, and sent children in one-by-one to **pick out** the box they liked best. Over twenty percent picked Sugar Boomers, a substantial market share.

Next, the mothers' discussion group. When asked to **comment on** a Sugar Boomers advertisement, **four out of five mothers** responded positively to the key phrase "free of vitamin additives." Also, our observers behind a one-way mirror counted twenty-seven smiles during the cartoon sequence.

Finally, the taste test. **As predicted,** the kide loved it. Most of them managed to eat two or three bowls before their mothers made them stop.

ADVICE

在對客戶做市調報告（market research）時，報告者必須先了解客戶的需求，再決定報告的內容是採取重點說明，還是詳細解說每一項步驟。通常在一開始即可點出調查的結果，以下再用各項調查方式來支持前面的結論。若基於調查結果有任何建議事項，可在結尾時提出。

市調報告

● 演說實例 ●

經過廣泛的市場調查之後，我們對新產品,「布媽媽早餐甜麥片」, 抱有很高的期望。

首先要報告的是購物模擬試驗的結果。在這項試驗當中, 我們用的是典型超級市場裏的物品架, 在上面放滿了各種早餐麥片, 然後讓小孩一個個進去, 挑選他們最喜歡的一盒。超過百分之二十的小孩挑選了「布媽媽甜麥片」, 這是相當大的市場佔有率。

其次, 是媽媽討論團。被問到對於「布媽媽甜麥片」廣告的意見時, 五分之四的媽媽對關鍵廣告詞,「不含維他命添加物」, 都有正面的反應。此外, 播放卡通片的時候, 我們的觀察員從單面的鏡子後面, 計算出有二十七個人在微笑。

最後, 是試吃。正如我們所料, 孩子們很愛吃。大部份的小孩, 到媽媽不准他們吃為止, 都已經吃了兩、三碗。

** extensive〔ɪkˈstɛnsɪv〕*adj.* 廣泛的　cereal〔ˈsɪrɪəl〕*n.* 麥片
simulation〔ˌsɪmjəˈleʃən〕*n.* 模擬
substantial〔səbˈstænʃəl〕*adj.* 相當大的；豐富的
respond〔rɪˈspɑnd〕*v.* 反應　positively〔ˈpɑzɪtɪvlɪ〕*adv.* 正面地；肯定地
vitamin〔ˈvaɪtəmɪn〕*n.* 維他命　additive〔ˈædətɪv〕*n.* 添加物
sequence〔ˈsikwəns〕*n.* 連續；系列（此指卡通的連續鏡頭）
bowl〔bol〕*n.* 碗

Useful Expressions

市調結果

1. We have high hopes for our new printer.

   我們對於新型印表機抱有很高的期望。

2. Our initial testing indicates that our new brand could be a winner.

   我們的初步試驗顯示，我們的新品牌可能會成為贏家。

3. *Two out of three* people responded positively.

   三分之二的人有正面的反應。

4. Over sixty percent *chose A over B.*

   百分之六十以上的人選 A，而不選 B。

5. The research shows that customers prefer a yellow package.

   調查指出，顧客比較喜歡黃色的包裝。

6. According to the survey, Brand X is considered inferior.

   根據調查，X 牌被認為是較差的牌子。

7. The questionnaire results are very promising.

   問卷調查結果顯示希望很大。

說明市調方法

1. We interviewed 50 people on the street randomly.

   我們在街頭抽樣訪問五十人。

** initial 〔ɪ'nɪʃəl〕 *adj.* 最初的
  indicate 〔'ɪndə,ket〕 *v.* 顯示   survey 〔'sɝve; sə've〕 *n.* 調查
  inferior 〔ɪn'fɪrɪɚ〕 *adj.* 較差的   questionnaire 〔,kwɛstʃən'ɛr〕 *n.* 問卷
  randomly 〔'rændəmlɪ〕 *adj.* 隨便地；無目的地

2. We asked some housewives to
   come over for a free testing
   of our new product.

我們邀請一些家庭主婦對我們的新產品作自由測試的訪問。

3. The product was test-marketed
   in ten cities **across the country.**

這項產品在全國十個城市作銷售試驗。

┃提出結論

1. We propose changing the color.

我們提議改變顏色。

2. We recommend a blue package.

我們建議用藍色包裝。

3. We concluded that the product
   contains too much sugar.

我們的結論是，這項產品含糖過高。

** propose〔prə'poz〕*v.* 提議
   recommend〔,rɛkə'mɛnd〕*v.* 建議；推薦

● 演說小教室 ●

　　國人在說英語時，常會有「**口音**」（accent）的煩惱，甚至因此而不敢開口。反觀美國大學中，來自非洲各國及印度的留學生卻都很有勇氣，以一口不甚標準的英語，活躍在各式場合中。他們很多都和國人一樣有很重的「口音（accent）」，但他們對發音上的細節問題一概不管。相反的，卻以明晰的**邏輯方式**貫徹自己的主張。雖說一口標準的美語值得我們學習，但有時候能夠說出自己的想法，比拘泥於發音或文法的細微處還來得重要。

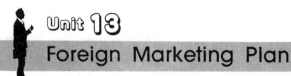

Unit 13
Foreign Marketing Plan

● A Sample Speech ●

I want to **inform** you **of** our plans to internationalize our market. Our conclusion is that we should **go ahead** and market our products overseas. The following are our three basic reasons.

First, our investigation reveals that there has not been much competition **so far** in the North American market **with regard to** these products. So there is still enough room for us to get in.

Second, our investigation also indicates that **the majority of American consumers** wish to buy this type of low-priced products which are not yet widely available in the United States.

Third, since we have accumulated a sufficient financial base to venture into the overseas market, we feel we ought to start marketing our products to the United States, and then to other parts of the world.

ADVICE

在向國外客戶或代理商說明公司的海外行銷調查結果時，可採取「先敘述結論，後申述理由」的方式。一份海外市場調查，宜從地域性的特徵著手；說明市場的多寡及占有率；再輔以公司的財力、人力狀況，加強客戶信心。

海外行銷計劃

● 演說實例 ●

　　我要告訴各位我們市場國際化的計畫。我們的結論是，我們應該進一步，把我們的產品行銷海外。以下是我們三點基本理由。

　　第一，我們的調查顯示，到目前為止，這類產品在北美市場的競爭還不太激烈。因此，還有足夠的空間讓我們進入。

　　第二，我們的調查，也顯示大多數的美國消費者希望購買這類低價位，而在美國尚未十分普遍的產品。

　　第三，由於我們已經累積了足夠的經濟基礎，可以進軍海外市場，所以我們覺得，應該開始把我們的產品行銷美國，然後再銷到世界其他地區。

**　internationalize〔͵ɪntɚˈnæʃənḷ͵aɪz〕*v.* 國際化
　investigation〔ɪn͵vɛstəˈgeʃən〕*n.* 調查　　***with regard to*** 關於
　accumulate〔əˈkjumjə͵let〕*v.* 累積　indicate〔ˈɪndə͵ket〕*v.* 顯示
　majority〔məˈdʒɔrətɪ, məˈdʒɑrətɪ〕*n.* 多數
　sufficient〔səˈfɪʃənt〕*adj.* 足夠的
　financial〔fəˈnæʃəl, faɪˈnænʃəl〕*adj.* 財務的
　venture〔ˈvɛntʃɚ〕*v.* 冒險

Useful Expressions

▌報告開場白

1. I would like to announce the results of our investigation about
   the marketability of our products
   in the U.S.

   我要宣布有關本公司產品,
   在美國的市場性調查的結果。

2. The investigating committee has
   reached its **final decision**.

   調查委員會已經達成最後的
   決定。

▌公布調查結果

1. After careful evaluation,we have
   reached the following conclusion.

   經過仔細的評估之後,我們
   已經達成以下的決定。

2. We have decided to **venture into**
   the international market.

   我們已經決定進軍國際市場。

3. We have **come to the conclusion**
   that there is a market for our
   products.

   我們的結論是,我們的產品
   有市場。

4. We have **arrived at a conclusion**
   to export our products in foreign markets **because of** the following reasons.

   由於下列原因,我們的結論
   是決定將產品外銷海外。

** committee 〔kə'mɪtɪ〕 *n.* 委員會
marketability 〔,mɑrkɪtə'bɪlətɪ〕 *n.* 市場性
evaluation 〔ɪ,væljʊ'eʃən〕 *n.* 評估

對調查結果的說明

1. One of the reasons for exporting is that our products are very competitive.

   外銷的原因之一是，我們的產品非常具有競爭力。

2. One of the reasons for not exporting is that similar products are already available overseas.

   不外銷的原因之一是，海外已經有類似的產品了。

3. We have a ready niche for our products.

   我們的產品有適當的市場。

4. There is really a need for this product in the international market.

   這項產品在國際市場上有實際的需要。

5. We've been approached several times by people abroad about marketing our products in their countries.

   我們已經和國外人士多次接洽過，有關我們的產品在他國的銷售事宜。

   ** niche〔nɪtʃ〕*n.* 適當的位置　　approach〔ə'protʃ〕*v.* 接洽

● **演說小教室** ●

　　開會時的座位安排會影響到聽眾在會議中的注意力、參與感及溝通結果。一般而言**寬而平面式**的排列方式較深而長的方式要好。如圖①的 **U 字排列**、圖②的**扇形排列**，就比圖③的方式理想，聽眾感覺較輕鬆，也沒有長形會議桌，聽眾和主席之間距離不一的缺點。此外，會議室中如果有窗戶，寧可安排主席面對窗戶，而不要讓聽眾因此而分散注意力。

圖①　　　　圖②　　　　　圖③

Unit 14
The New Branch Abroad

● A Sample Speech ●

Ladies and gentlemen, it is a great pleasure to have all of you join us as we open our plant here in Springfield.

Some of you may **be concerned about** working for a foreign owned company. Let me just say that in my country, we **take** great **pride in** how well we treat our employees.

We **believe** in providing job security, good pay and benefits, and good working conditions. We will do our best to make you feel comfortable working for us, and we expect you to do your best **in return**. Thank you.

ADVICE

這篇演講由三個部分構成。第一是歡迎辭,第二是關於公司給予員工的各項福利。第三是有關公司向員工的要求。這是一篇 Give and take 邏輯的演講。在開設分公司和工廠時,除了清楚地說明公司給予員工的利益外,也要強調企業所要求的工作態度和熱愛公司的精神。

成立海外分公司

● 演說實例 ●

各位女士，各位先生，我們在春田設立工廠，承蒙各位加入，令我們感到非常高興。

各位當中，或許有人對於在外國人的公司工作，感到擔憂。讓我告訴各位，在我國我們對待員工非常好，這一點我們覺得很自豪。

我們深信我們應該提供工作保障，優厚的待遇和福利，以及良好的工作條件。我們會盡全力來讓各位覺得在這裏工作很舒適；同樣的，我們也希望各位能夠盡全力在工作上回饋，謝謝！

** security〔sɪˈkjʊrətɪ〕*n.* 安全保障　benefit〔ˈbɛnəfɪt〕*n.* 福利
in return 以爲報答

Useful Expressions

開場白

1. We are very happy to open a new branch in Seattle.

能在西雅圖設立新的分公司,我們感到非常高興。

2. It is a great pleasure to establish a new branch here in St. Louis.

能夠在聖路易設立新的分公司,是我們莫大的榮幸。

3. We are all very excited about opening this brand-new factory.

我們對於這家新工廠的創立,都感到非常興奮。

提到兩國間的交流

1. If we combine Chinese diligence with American creativity, anything is possible.

如果我們結合中國人的勤奮和美國人的創造力,那就沒有辦不到的事。

2. We will *do our best* to make this factory comfortable.

我們會盡力使各位在工廠裏感到舒適。

3. If you *are confused by* the Chinese way of management, please *talk* it *over* with us.

如果各位對中國式的經營有不清楚的地方,請找我們討論。

4. We want you to be proud of working for us.

我們要各位以為我們工作為傲。

5. The success of this branch really *depends upon* each of you.

這家分公司的成功實需仰賴各位。

** brand-new 〔'brænd'n(j)u〕 *adj.* 全新的   combine 〔kəm'baɪn〕 *v.* 結合
diligence 〔'dɪlədʒəns〕 *n.* 勤勉   confuse 〔kən'fjuz〕 *v.* 困擾;使混亂

● 演說小教室 ●

　　如果是祝賀外商公司進入台灣市場，可以在演說中提出**具體的事實**，如「雇用本地的員工」，來說明有助於台灣經濟發展及中美雙方文化交流。

　　I am very happy that you have finally established a branch in Taipei. Your presence here will be a great contribution to the local business community as a whole. I understand that the majority of employees here are Chinese, and I think you have made the right decision, because such constructive employment practices will greatly promote a better understanding of both American and Chinese cultures.

　　I wish you the best of luck in your new venture, and also hope you will be able to make a unique contribution to the economy of both countries.

　　我很高興你們終於在台北設立了分公司，你們的加入就整體來說，對本地商界將是一大貢獻。我知道在此地大多數的員工都是中國人，而且我認為你們的決定是對的，因為如此有建設性的就業策略將更有助於中美雙方文化的了解。

　　祝福你們的新計畫一帆風順，也希望你們能對兩國間的經濟都有特殊的貢獻。

** contribution〔͵kɑntrəˈbjuʃən〕*n.* 貢獻
community〔kəˈmjunətɪ〕*n.* 團體
constructive〔kənˈstrʌktɪv〕*adj.* 建設性的
practice〔ˈpræktɪs〕*n.* 策略；實施
economy〔ɪˈkɑnəmɪ; iˈkɑnəmɪ〕*n.* 經濟

數字英語②

★ 分數

3分之2	two thirds
2分之1	a [one] half
4分之1	a [one] fourth [quarter]

★ 年月日

752	seven [hundred and] fifty-two
1986	nineteen eighty-six
1800	eighteen hundred
5月1日	1st May (the first of May) (英)
	May 1st (May [the] first (one)) (美)

★ 金額

$ 15.25	fifteen dollars [and] twenty-five [cents]
£ 3.50	three pounds [and] fifty [pence]

★ 算式

2＋3＝5	Two plus three equals five.
	Two and three is (are) five.
5－2＝3	Five minus two equals three.
	Two from five leaves three.
2×3＝6	Two multiplied by three equals six.
	Two times three is six.
6÷2＝3	Six divided by two equals three.
	Two goes into six three times.

Chapter

4

即席專題演說
Persuasive
Speeches

Unit 1
Chinese Attitude toward Work

● A Sample Speech ●

Well, I promised to **give a speech** about Chinese attitudes toward work, but I'm not sure where to begin. **On the one hand,** I could talk about the Confucian work ethic. **On the other hand,** I could mention all the ways in which people from Taiwan have tried to " get rich quick." Sometimes its hard to tell where Chinese culture ends and human nature begins.

Perhaps the best thing would be to point out a few contrasts between the Chinese and other people. For example, many Westerners assume that Chinese working habits are the same as Japanese; but this is not true at all. For Chinese people, the family is the center of their lives, not the company, and they value their leisure time very highly.

To sum up, the Chinese have about the same attitudes toward work as anybody else. Only the system is slightly different.

ADVICE

中國人一向被世人認爲是個勤奮節儉的民族，但近年來國際間對台灣這個「貪婪之島」（Island of Avarice）上的暴發戶心態也充滿好奇。但要在二、三分鐘內說明國人的工作觀，也不太容易，在開頭概略地提一下問題的多面性，再採取中美或中日「比較」（comparison）的方法；也是一種技巧。

國人的工作觀

● 演說實例 ●

　　嗯，我答應過要談談中國人的工作態度，可是我不知道要從哪裏說起。一方面，我可以談談儒家的工作倫理；另一方面，我也可以說說台灣人想「迅速致富」的所有方法。有時候，中國文化和人性的界線，是很難畫分清楚的。

　　可能最好的方法，是指出中國人和其他國家人民之間的不同處。舉例來說，許多西方人以為中國人的工作習慣和日本人相同，可是事實並非如此。對中國人而言，生活的重心是家庭，不是公司。同時，中國人也非常注重休閒時間。

　　總之，中國人的工作態度和其他人大同小異，只不過制度稍有不同罷了。

** attitude〔ˊætə,tjud〕 *n.* 態度　　***on the one hand*** 一方面
　　Confucian〔kənˊfjuʃən〕 *adj.* 儒家的　　ethic〔ˊɛθɪk〕 *n.* 倫理
　　contrast〔ˊkɑntræst〕 *n.* 差別；對比　assume〔əˊsjum, əˊsum〕 *v.* 以為

Useful Expressions

開場白

1. Let me describe how our work attitudes **differ from** Americans'.

讓我來描述一下，我們的工作態度和美國人有何不同。

2. I am going to explain why most people in Taiwan work so hard.

我要解釋一下,為什麼台灣大部分的人都這麼賣力地工作。

3. Let me briefly discuss some of tne differences between the Chinese and the Americans when it comes to work.

讓我簡短地談談，中國人和美國人在工作時，有什麼不同的地方。

國人的工作觀

1. We **view** work **as** an essential factor in becoming part of a community.

我們視工作為成為社會一份子的要素。

2. Work gives us **a sense of belonging** in a community.

工作給予我們對社會的歸屬感。

3. These days, our views on work are changing.

最近我們對於工作的看法正在改變中。

4. The younger generation is not as job-oriented as the older generations.

年輕一代已不像老一輩那樣以工作為重心。

** essential 〔ə'sɛnʃəl〕 *adj.* 最重要的
belonging 〔bɪ'lɔŋɪŋ〕 *n.* 歸屬
orient 〔'orɪ,ɛnt,'ɔr-〕 *v.* 朝向；使順應

5. A sense of loyalty to the company seems to be disappearing rapidly.

對於公司的忠誠度似乎正迅速地消失當中。

6. Many young people in Taiwan now have several part-time jobs instead of just one-full time job.

現在台灣許多年輕人擁有多份兼職的工作，而非只有一份全職的工作。

7. Whether or not one is employed is *a matter of face* to most Chinese.

對多數中國人而言，會不會被僱用是面子問題

┃中美工作觀比較

1. The American work ethic seems to be more individualistic.

美國人的工作倫理似乎是比較個人主義的。

2. Americans often value results and accomplishments *more than* processes.

美國人重視結果和成就遠勝於過程。

3. The Chinese work for group goals while Americans work for individual goals.

中國人爲團體目標而工作，而美國人卻爲個人目的而工作。

** loyalty 〔ˈlɔɪəltɪ, ˈlɔj-〕 *n.* 忠誠
individualistic 〔ˌɪndəˌvɪdʒʊəˈlɪstɪk, -dʒʊl-〕 *adj.* 個人主義的
value 〔ˈvæljʊ〕 *v.* 重視　　rough 〔rʌf〕 *adj.* 概略的

● 演說小敎室 ●

　　幽默的演講可以帶給聽眾輕鬆的氣氛並集中聽眾的注意力。但卽使用中文，要講出幽默的演說，也不是件容易的事，英語就更不用說了。

　　那麼如何才能發表幽默的演講呢？就是適當地用「**諺語**」、「**名言**」和「**比喻**」。首先背一些英語的慣用句，再配合演講的內容去構思，就可以說出一篇幽默的演講了。

Unit 2
Protectionism

● A Sample Speech ●

Opening up our markets is something we totally **agree with** you about. We are going to do this **not only because** the United States government is asking us to do so **but** also **because** it makes good economic sense.

Creating a more liberal economy should **first of all** make life more affordable to our people as cheaper goods and services are one of the consequences of a less restrictive economy. Letting market forces operate more freely should also make our industries leaner and more efficient. Only with direct global competition can we ensure the continued growth and development of our economy. We also understand that in order for the world trading system to continue functioning well, we should strive to become more responsible players.

The ROC government **is committed to** unshackling the economy but we need time to **make the adjustments**. A rush into liberalization will only create chaos and disruptions in our economy which **in turn** will not **be in the best interests** of everyone concerned.

ADVICE

近年來台灣一直標榜著貿易自由化（liberalize）與國際化（internationalize），但在面對美國保護主義（Protectionism）的指責之下，又顯得站不住腳。因此在說明這個現象時，可採取迂迴戰術，一方面列舉日本做為擋箭牌，一方面則說明政府仍具改善誠意，只是基於國內因素,採取較緩和的速度開放市場。

保護主義

● 演說實例 ●

　　我們完全贊同開放我們的國內市場，而且我們也將朝這個方向努力，不單是因為來自美國的壓力，也是因為開放市場才是一個良好的經濟政策。

　　首先，開創一個更自由的經濟體系可使人民的生活較寬裕，因為一個限制較少的經濟體系，能提供較便宜的商品與服務。而且讓市場更自由地運作，也可使我國的企業更加精簡而有效率。唯有與全球市場直接競爭，才能確保我們經濟的穩定成長。我們也了解，為了維持世界經濟體系正常運作，我們應該更有責任感。

　　中華民國政府相當有誠意要開放經濟市場，但我們需要時間去調適。急進的邁向自由市場只會造成我國經濟的混亂與瓦解，這必然也不是大家所希望的。

** consequence〔'kɑnsə,kwɛns〕*n.* 結果　restrictive〔rɪ'strɪktɪv〕*adj.* 限制的
lean〔lin〕*adj.* 瘦的；精瘦的（在此為去除冗弊，更加精簡之意）
strive〔starv〕*v.* 努力；奮鬥　　commit〔kə'mɪt〕*v.* 委託
be committed 給予承諾　unshackle〔ʌn'ʃækl̩〕*v.* 釋放；除去～的枷鎖
adjustment〔ə'dʒʌstmənt〕*n.* 調適
rush〔rʌʃ〕*n.* 急進　disruption〔dɪs'rʌpʃən〕*n.* 瓦解
chaos〔'keɑs〕*n.* 紛亂；混亂

Useful Expressions

表明立場

1. We realize the importance of being a fair player in the world trading system.

我們了解在世界貿易中，公平競爭的重要性。

2. The ROC's tariff rates are now *comparable to* those found in industrialized nations.

中華民國的關稅和工業化國家的稅率相當。

3. Taiwan has done a lot *in terms of* opening its markets.

台灣對開放市場已做了很多努力。

4. We have done more than say South Korea or other country in liberalizing our tax laws.

在開放稅法方面，我們做得比南韓或其他國家更多。

5. We do not like *being targeted as* an unfair trading partner.

我們不希望被認為是不公平的貿易夥伴。

6. Freeing the economy to foreign competition takes some time.

開放外來競爭的自由經濟需要一些時間。

7. Opening up the market will definitely make goods more affordable to a lot of consumers.

市場的開放的確會使大多消費者更有能力購買物品。

** tariff〔'tærɪf〕*n.* 關稅；稅率   *in terms of* 以～的方式
liberalize〔'lɪbərəl,aɪz,'lɪbrəl-〕*v.* 開放；自由化
target〔'tɑrgɪt〕*v.* 定目標   definitely〔'dɛfənɪtlɪ〕*adv.* 明確地
affordable〔ə'fordəbḷ, ə'fɔrdəbḷ〕*adj.* 有能力的

提出呼籲

1. At any rate, the R.O.C. and the United States need each other, and we have to maintain communication to understand each other.

無論如何，中華民國和美國相互需要，我們必須保持溝通以了解彼此。

2. The U.S. government and industries should not *put all the blame on* the R.O.C., but open talk to improve the trade imbalance.

美國政府和工業界不應全然歸咎中華民國，而應該開始以談判來改善貿易逆差。

3. Both the R.O.C. and the United States should realize there is no immediate solution to the trade issues.

中美雙方都應了解，對於貿易問題並沒有立即的解決之道。

4. The US and Taiwan should work together in trying open the Japanese market.

美國和台灣應合作共同打開日本市場。

** imbalance〔ɪmˈbæləns〕*n.* 不平衡
solution〔səˈluʃən, səˈljuʃən〕*n.* 解決
issue〔ˈɪʃʊ, -ʃjʊ〕*n.* 論點

● 演說小教室 ●

諺語雖可表示真理，但用得不恰當便會成為陳腔爛調，使用者必須下一番工夫，此外，**不要把諺語拿來當結論**，因為用陳腔爛調做結論，會抹剎了你前面所要表達的想法。

善於使用諺語的秘訣是，把諺語當做演講內容的**補充材料**，而且可以把諺語稍微**變化**一下。譬如想要讚美某人非常有手腕時，可以很幽默地說："People say, 'we can kill two birds with one stone.' But he killed three!"（「人家說『一石二鳥』，但是他可以一石三鳥。」

Unit 3

Threats from NIES

● A Sample Speech ●

Over the last five years, our company has faced increasing competition from NIES (Newly Industrializing Economies), particularly Korea. This is partly **due to** the rising NT dollar, which has made our products more expensive overseas. Skyrocketing labor costs are another important factor. How can we **cope with** being undersold?

Our solution is to switch to more sophisticated products where Taiwan has an advantage. This will require an intensive R&D effort on our part. However, we have plenty of computer engineers, and the government is willing to underwrite a large amount of research work. There is every reason to be optimistic.

By upgrading our products, we can avoid competition from other Asian countries, as well as **take advantage of** Taiwan's vast resources in the information industry.

ADVICE

台灣的經濟受到其它亞洲新興工業國家（NIES）的負面影響，是個不爭的事實。因此在公開場合被問及這項威脅時，演說者在開頭可先提一下整個大環境所受的威脅，本論中再縮小範圍，說明公司的因應之道。

新興工業國家的威脅

● 演說實例 ●

　　過去五年以來，我們公司面臨了其他新興工業國家愈來愈激烈的競爭，尤其是韓國。這種情況的部份原因來自台幣升值，使我們的產品在國外比較昂貴。工資激漲也是另一個重要因素。我們怎麼處理其他國家的商品售價比我們低的問題？

　　我們的解決方法是開始生產對台灣有利，且較為精密的產品。這需要我們在研究及開發方面投注密集的心力。不過，我們有許多電腦工程師，而政府也保證願意支付大量研究工作的經費，我們應該是很樂觀的。

　　藉著產品升級，我們可以避免其他亞洲國家的競爭，也可以好好利用台灣資訊業的廣大資源。

**　skyrocketing〔ˈskaɪˌrɑkɪtɪŋ〕*adj.* 猛漲的
　undersell〔ˌʌndɚˈsɛl〕*v.* 廉價出售　　switch〔swɪtʃ〕*v.* 轉變
　underwrite〔ˌʌndɚˈraɪt〕*v.* 保證；承諾
　sophisticated〔səˈfɪstɪˌketɪd〕*adj.* 精密的
　optimistic〔ˌɑptəˈmɪstɪk〕*adj.* 樂觀的

Useful Expressions

問題所在

1. Taiwan is not competitive anymore when it comes to *labor
   intensive industries.*

   在勞工密集工業方面，台灣
   已不再具有競爭力了。

2. Newly Industrializing Economies such
   as Korea, Singapore and mainland
   China have been becoming more and
   more competitive in recent years.

   新興工業國家，如韓國，新
   加坡和中國大陸，在近幾年
   來越來越具有競爭力。

3. Our Asian competitors are now
   trying to undercut us.

   我們亞洲的同業正試圖開出
   比我們更低的價格。

因應之道

1. We have to *divert* some of our
   attention *towards* the local market.

   我們必須將注意力轉到本土
   市場上。

2. We are lucky to have the government supporting us.

   我們很幸運有政府的支持。

3. We'll try to tap the European market.

   我們將設法取得歐洲市場。

4. We have to improve our quality.

   我們必須改良我們的品質。

5. R&D is essential to our sur-
   vival.

   「研究發展」對我們的生存
   是很重要的。

** intensive 〔ɪn'tɛnsɪv〕 *adj.* 密集的
   undercut 〔͵ʌndə'kʌt〕 *v.* 索價低於（他人）
   divert 〔də'vɝt, daɪ-〕 *v.* 轉向　　tap 〔tæp〕 *v.* 獲取
   R&D 研究發展（*research & development*）

6. We have to make more *value-added products*.

我們必須生產更多有附加價值的產品。

7. Streamlining our operations may be the answer.

提高我們的作業效率也許是答案。

8. Making our production processes more efficient will help cut costs.

提高我們生產過程的效率有助於降低成本。

9. A service mentality will help us keep our customers.

服務心理會幫助我們留住顧客。

結論

1. We look at this as a challenge.

我們視此為一項挑戰。

2. We'll *make it* through the transition.

我們會順利地通過這段過渡時期。

3. We should not underestimate them, but watch *with caution* how they perform in business and trade.

我們不應低估他們，而要謹慎地觀察他們在企業和貿易上如何運作。

** streamline〔'strim,laɪn〕*v.* 提高效率　mentality〔mɛn'tælətɪ〕*n.* 心理狀態
challenge〔'tʃælɪndʒ〕*n.* 挑戰　　　transition〔træn'zɪʃən〕*n.* 過渡
underestimate〔'ʌndɚ'ɛstə,met〕*v.* 低估　　caution〔'kɔʃən〕*n.* 謹慎

●─── 演說小教室 ●───

在演講中使用**諺語**（Proverb），可以產生許多效果。第一，諺語中含有幾分真實，可帶來說服力。其次，諺語可簡明扼要地表示**抽象意義**，又可避免冗長又單調的演說。此外，在英語演講中引用諺語，可以表示出自己的英語程度。

不過，必須「**適當地**」使用。譬如："A rolling stone gathers no moss.（滾石不生苔）"這個諺語，在英國是給人負面的印象，而在美國則有正面的含意。

Unit 4
Local Investment Environment

● A Sample Speech ●

I would like to introduce you to **investment opportunities** in Taiwan. Now many of you are probably chuckling to yourselves. You're probably thinking about all the crazy people at the **stock exchange**. But Taiwan is not really all like that.

Most Taiwan companies are not even listed on the stock exchange, for obvious reasons. Yet they can be remarkably stable and productive. Our company is a good example.

The fact is that Taiwan is one of the most hospitable environments for business in all of Asia. Our government is not only quite stable, it has consistently adopted pro-business policies **with respect to** taxation, regulation, and so on.

Come **take advantage of** the " Taiwan miracle" and invest in our country.

ADVICE

由於台灣股市的不正常現象及社會治安問題，導致許多外商公司對投資望而怯步。在此你可以採用「以退爲進」的策略，先指出許多不利外商投資的現象，如股市熱，著作法等；再逐項修正這些錯誤觀念及改進成果，最後提出各項優惠外商投資的條件，呼籲外商繼續投資。

簡介國內投資環境

● 演說實例 ●

　　我想向各位介紹台灣的投資機會。講到這裏,各位可能會暗笑,並想到股票市場那些瘋狂的人潮。但是並非整個台灣都是像這樣的。

　　由於一些很明顯的原因,台灣大部份公司,並未上市股票。但是,這些公司也有非常穩定,生產力很強的。本公司就是個很好的例子。

　　事實上,台灣是全亞洲最好客的企業環境之一。我們的政府不僅相當穩定,更是不斷在稅制、法規等方面採行對企業有利的政策。

　　趕緊把握「台灣奇蹟」的機會,到我們國家來投資。

** chuckle〔'tʃʌkḷ〕*v.* 暗自發笑　　　*stock exchange* 證券交易所
obvious〔'abvɪəs〕*adj.* 顯然的　　remarkably〔rɪ'mɑrkəblɪ〕*adv.* 非常地
hospitable〔'haspɪtəbḷ〕*adj.* 慇懃的;好客的
adopt〔ə'dɑpt〕*v.* 採行;採用　　　*with respect to* 關於
taxation〔tæks'eʃən〕*n.* 課稅　　　miracle〔'mɪrəkḷ〕*n.* 奇蹟

Useful Expressions

談及國際間的誤解

1. Taiwan has always *been known as* a heaven for intellectual pirates.

   台灣一直被認為是盜版的天堂。

2. We used to *supply* the world *with* cheap, low quality products.

   我們以前曾供應全球低價的次級貨品。

3. We now have a Taiwan different from the one you knew five or ten years ago.

   現在的台灣，已不同於你們五年或十年前所認識的台灣。

4. Taiwan is no longer a maker of cheap, low-quality products.

   台灣不再是廉價次級貨品的製造者了。

糾正錯誤觀念

1. The pace of democratic change is quickening.

   民主政治改革的腳步正在加快當中。

2. The government is trying to *bring* underground black market businesses *out into the light*.

   政府正努力使地下黑市企業合法化。

3. Liberalization and internationalization are now key concepts in our economic policies.

   自由化和國際化是我們目前經濟政策的首要觀念。

** pirate〔'paɪrət〕*n.* 盜印（書籍）；盜製（唱片、錄音帶等）
pace〔pes〕*n.* 走或跑的速度　liberalization〔‚lɪbərəlaɪ'zeʃən〕*n.* 自由化
internationalization〔‚ɪntɚ‚næʃənlə'zeʃən,-aɪ'ze-〕*n.* 國際化
concept〔'kɑnsɛpt〕*n.* 觀念

4. We are rapidly making the transition into a mature industrialized country.

我們會很快地轉型，成為一個成熟的工業化國家。

5. This country is no longer a third world country.

這個國家已不再是個第三世界的國家。

6. There's no need to be alarmed about Taiwan's social order.

不須對台灣的社會安全感到恐慌。

提出呼籲

1. The country remains a favorite among foreign investors.

這個國家仍是外國投資者的最愛。

2. Investment in Taiwan is still worthwhile.

在台灣的投資仍然是值得的。

3. We can guarantee a lucrative return on your investment.

我們可以保證，你們的投資絕對會獲利。

** transition〔træn'zɪʃən, -s'ɪʃən〕 *n.* 轉型；轉變
  alarm〔ə'lɑrm〕 *v.* 使恐慌　lucrative〔'lukrətɪv〕 *adj.* 獲利的

● 演說小教室 ●

1. Haste makes waste. 欲速則不達。
2. Easy come, easy go. 賺得容易花的快。
3. Birds of a feather flock together. 物以類聚。
4. Business is business. 公事公辦。
5. Still waters run deep. 靜水深流。
6. Like father, like son. 有其父必有其子。
7. A bird in the hand is worth two in the bush. 一鳥在手勝於二鳥在林。
8. A drowning man will crasp at a straw. 狗急跳牆。
9. Let bygones be bygones. 既往不咎。
10. The pen is mightier than the sword. 文勝於武。

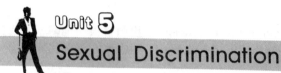

Unit 5
Sexual Discrimination

• A Sample Speech •

It has been quite some time since women entered the labor market in Taiwan.

As to our company, we have a policy of doing everything we can to support women managers. Currently we have three female vice presidents, and over forty percent of our senior officers are women.

We offer generous **maternity leave,** as well as **on-site day care** facilities. Sexual discrimination or harassment of any kind **is subject to** strict disciplinary action.

By helping women managers reach their full potential, we can ensure that our company need never lack for competent leadership. Equality is something we cannot afford NOT to have. Thank you.

ADVICE

台灣婦女的地位比起鄰國的日本、韓國，可謂居全亞洲之冠。因此被問及有關性別歧視（sexual discrimiation）的問題時，可從台灣女性就業市場、公司雇用女性員工的原則與福利三方面著手。

性別歧視

● 演說實例 ●

　　在台灣，婦女加入勞工市場已有一段時間了。

　　至於我們公司，我們有一個既定政策，那就是盡力支持女性經理。目前，我們有三位女性副總經理，而我們的高級主管中超過百分之四十是女性。

　　我們提供優厚的產假，並在公司裏設有白天托兒的設施。任何的性別歧視及性騷擾都會受到嚴格的處罰。

　　藉著幫助女性經理充分發揮潛能，我們可以確定，本公司絕對不會缺乏領導人才。兩性平等是我們堅持的宗旨，謝謝！

** maternity〔məˊtɝnətɪ〕*adj.* 懷孕的　　***maternity leave*** 產假
on-site day care facility 白天托兒的設備
discrimination〔dɪ,skrɪməˊneʃən〕*n.* 歧視
harassment〔həˊræsmənt〕*n.* 騷擾　　***be subject to*** 受制於⋯的
disciplinary〔ˊdɪsəplɪn,ɛrɪ〕*adj.* 懲戒的　　ensure〔ɪnˊʃʊr〕*v.* 保證
competent〔ˊkɑmpətənt〕*adj.* 能幹的

Useful Expressions

▎台灣女性就業情形

1. In Taiwan, more and more women are becoming career-oriented.

   在台灣，越來越多的婦女以工作為重心。

2. Women in Taiwan have received enough education, and **are equipped with** the necessary skills and training to **compete** equally **with** men.

   台灣婦女已接受了足夠的教育，有了必備的技術和訓練與男性公平競爭。

3. More and more women are entering the workforce here in Taiwan.

   在台灣，愈來愈多的婦女進入就職市場。

4. Women **are** now more **conscious of** their rights.

   現代婦女較能意識到她們的權利。

▎公司尊重女性員工的聲明

1. We support equal pay for equal work.

   我們支持同工同酬。

2. Thanks to women's liberation, business is no longer a "good old boy" system.

   由於婦女解放運動，企業界已不再是男士們的天下。

3. We take charges of **sexual harassment** very seriously.

   我們非常注意性騷擾事件。

4. We believe we should do our best to encourage women's participation in business enterprises.

   我們相信盡該盡力鼓勵女性加入企業界。

** workforce〔'wɝk,fors〕 *n.* 勞動力　　repeal〔rɪ'pil〕 *v.* 廢止
conscious〔'kɑnʃəs〕 *adj.* 有意識的　　liberation〔,lɪbə'reʃən〕 *n.* 解放
enterprise〔'ɛntɚ,praɪz〕 *n.* 企業

針對女性員工的政策

1. We have removed all *sexist language* in all our company communications.

在公司所有的溝通方式中，我們排除所有蔑視女性的語言。

2. Women here enjoy the same pay scale as men.

女性和男性享有同樣的工資等級。

3. We are trying to increase the number of women managers in our company.

我們公司正試圖增加女性主管的人數。

** *sexist language* 蔑視女性的語言

● 演說小教室 ●

1. The proof of the pudding is in the eating. 行而後知成敗。

2. Where there's a will, there's a way. 有志者，事竟成。

3. Jack of all trades and master of none.
   樣樣懂，樣樣不精。（樣樣通樣樣稀鬆。）

4. So many men, so many minds. 人多主意多。

5. A sound mind in a sound body. 健全的心靈寓於健康的身體。

6. Everybody's business is nobody's business.
   衆人的事沒人管。

7. A stitch in time saves nine. 及時的一針，勝過九針。

8. All work and no play makes Jack a dull boy.
   只管用功不去玩，聰明孩子也變蠢。

9. Seeing is believing. 眼見為憑。

10. Strike the iron while it is hot. 打鐵趁熱。

Unit 6
Chinese & American Management

• A Sample Speech •

As many of you have undoubtedly noticed, our company's management philosophy is a little different from that of most American firms. Let me go over some of the differences with you.

First of all, we **emphasize cooperation over competition**. Where U.S. salesmen are usually paid by commission, ours are on a fixed salary. That way we **make sure** everyone works **as a team**.

Another difference is that we like to promote managers from within the company rather than bringing them in from outside. We believe that most people **prefer to** work under someone whom they know and respect, someone who knows the company.

Third, in our company, everyone's opinion is valued, and no decision is made without consulting everyone involved. **After all**, people are our most important asset.

ADVICE

這是一篇運用「比較法」的例子。在開場白之後,即逐項點出差異所在;每一段只比較一個不同點,並接著提出理由(reason)。在提出理由時,注意理由和不同點之間要有因果關係,才能合乎外國人的邏輯思考習慣。

中美管理方式

● 演說實例 ●

　　各位當中一定有很多人都注意到，我們公司的經營哲學，和大部份的美國公司有一點不太一樣。就讓我跟大家談談這些不同之處。

　　首先，我們重視合作甚於競爭。在美國，業務員通常是領取佣金，而我們的業務員則領取固定的薪水。這樣，我們才能確使大家保持團隊合作。

　　另一個不同點是，我們喜歡擢升公司的員工當經理，而不用空降部隊。我們相信，大部份的人都比較喜歡在他們認識、尊敬，而又了解公司的人底下工作。

　　第三，在我們公司裏，每個人的意見都受到尊重；一件事情在徵詢每一個有關人員的意見之前，是不會做決定的。畢竟，人力是我們最重要的資產。

** philosophy〔fə'lɑsəfɪ〕*n.* 哲學　　emphasize〔'ɛmfə,saɪz〕*v.* 強調
　 commission〔kə'mɪʃən〕*n.* 佣金　　consult〔kən'sʌlt〕*v.* 諮詢
　 asset〔'æsɛt〕*n.* 資產

Useful Expressions

比較

1. *As far as I know*, American management emphasizes efficiency, competition among workers, and top-down decision-making.

就我所知，美國式管理強調效率，同事之間的競爭，及上對下的決策。

2. The Chinese way of management is characterized by the seniority system and welfare guarantees.

中式管理是以年資制度和福利保證爲特色。

3. The American way of management features strong management leadership and unionism.

美式管理的特色則爲強大的管理領導權及工會制度。

4. *For instance*, workers of top companies can usually get a large sum of money for their *retirement allowance*.

例如，頂尖公司的員工通常可得到一筆爲數不小的退休金。

5. Personal liability figures heavily in American companies while liability as a group figures more in Chinese companies.

在美國公司中，個人的責任扮演很重要的角色，然而，在中國公司裏，群體的責任較爲重要。

** liability 〔͵laɪə'bɪlətɪ〕 *n.* 義務；責任
efficiency 〔ə'fɪʃənsɪ, ɪ-〕 *n.* 效率　　seniority 〔sin'jɔrətɪ〕 *n.* 年資
feature 〔'fitʃə〕 *v.* 以～爲特色　　unionism 〔'junjənɪzm̩〕 *n.* 工會主義
allowance 〔ə'lauəns〕 *n.* 津貼

6. A lot of companies in Taiwan are basically *family type* businesses, with outsiders having no chance to take *a crack at* the top.

很多台灣公司基本上是家族企業型態，外人根本沒有機會爬到最高位。

總結

1. It is difficult to decide which one is better.

很難定論哪一種方式較好。

2. There are some merits and demerits to both types of management.

兩種管理方式各有利弊。

3. My suggestion is that people of both countries should learn from each other.

我的建言是兩國人民應相互學習。

** crack 〔kræk〕 *n.* 打破
merit 〔'mɛrɪt〕 *n.* 優點　　demerit 〔di'mɛrɪt〕 *n.* 缺點

● 演說小教室 ●

1. Time and tide wait for no man. 歲月不待人。
2. First come first served. 捷足先登。
3. You cannot have your cake and eat it too. 魚與熊掌，不可兼得。
4. Let sleeping dogs lie. 別自找麻煩。
5. Out of sight, out of mind. 久離則疏遠。
6. In wine there is truth. 酒後吐真言。
7. Easier said than done. 說來容易做來難。
8. Actions speak louder than words. 行動勝於空談。
9. Live and learn. 活到老學到老。
10. All's well that ends well. 善終為善。

Unit 7
The Labor Shortage

• A Sample Speech •

Along with many other companies in Taiwan, we face an acute shortage of labor. Part of the problem is that many workers have lost sight of the value of hard work. Some of them are jobjumpers who quit one job after another. Others spend all day at the stock exchange trying to **make money** the easy way **instead of** the hard way.

As I see it, we have twe choices. One is to raise wages. However, **in the long run** this would tend to make our products less competitive.

Our other option is to **make use of** foreign labor. While hiring foreign workers is technically illegal, we can always relocate parts of our operations overseas.

Our labor problem will not go away **on its own,** but will only grow worse with time. It would behoove us to act sooner **rather than** later.

ADVICE

外國客戶可能會注意到台灣目益嚴重的「勞工短缺」問題，因此你的回答正提供了外國客戶判斷公司是否仍具競爭力的依據。誠懇地提出公司的因應之道是說服客戶最好的方法。至於一些會自曝其短的負面現象，可視場合避重就輕。

勞工短缺

● 演説實例 ●

　　跟台灣許多其他的公司一樣，我們面臨了嚴重的勞工短缺問題。這個問題有一部份是因為許多勞工已經無視於努力工作的價值了。他們有些是跳槽專家，工作一個接一個地換。其他則是整天待在號子裏，只想用輕鬆的方法賺錢，而不想努力。

　　依我看來，我們有兩種選擇。一種是提高工資。但是，從長遠的角度看來，這會降低我們產品的競爭力。

　　我們的另一個選擇是利用外籍勞工。雖然純粹就法律而言，僱用外籍勞工是非法的，但是我們總是可以把我們的部份作業移轉到海外去。

　　我們的勞工問題並不會自動消失，只會隨著時間日益惡化。早點採取行動，將對我們有利。

** acute 〔əˋkjut〕 *adj.* 嚴重的　　shortage 〔ˋʃɔrtɪdʒ〕 *n.* 短缺
job-jumper 〔dʒɑbˋdʒʌmpə〕 *n.* 跳槽者　　quit 〔kwɪt〕 *v.* 離職
wage 〔wedʒ〕 *n.* 工資　　illegal 〔ɪˋligl̩〕 *adj.* 非法的
relocate 〔riˋloket〕 *v.* 徙置於另一新地方
operation 〔͵ɑpəˋreʃən〕 *n.* 作業　behoove 〔bɪˋhuv〕 *v.* 有益於

Useful Expressions

突顯問題

1. Taiwan *suffers from* a shortage of manpower.

   台灣深受人力缺乏之苦。

2. Many employees have left their jobs to play money games.

   許多員工放下工作，而沈迷於金錢遊戲。

3. The labor structure of the country is changing.

   全國的勞動結構正在改變。

4. The service industry is attracting more workers *at the expense of* the industrial and agricultural sectors.

   服務業吸引了更多的勞工，卻犧牲了工業和農業。

5. The labor shortage has led many companies to go abroad.

   勞工短缺導致了許多公司遷移到國外。

6. Many companies have closed down *due to* the labor shortage.

   許多公司由於勞工短缺而被迫倒閉。

因應之道

1. Better management techniques should be adopted to retain employees.

   應採取更好的經營技巧來留住員工。

2. Computerizing your operation will save you a lot *in terms of* labor costs.

   電腦化作業可節省一大筆勞動成本。

** structure〔'strʌktʃə〕*n.* 結構　　*at the expense of* 犧牲
retain〔rɪ'ten〕*v.* 留住　computerize〔kəm'pjutə,raɪz〕*v.* 電腦化

3. The labor shortage has led to increases in workers' salaries.

勞工短缺導致了勞工薪資的提高。

4. Many workers are returning to the labor market after the *Stock Market Crash*.

在股票市場崩盤之後，許多工人又會回到勞動市場。

結論

1. Higher paying jobs at high-tech industries will sound the death knell for labor-intensive industries here.

高科技工業的高薪工作意味著此地勞力密集工業的死亡。

2. Using industrial robots is the only way out.

使用工業用機器人是唯一的解決之道。

3. The shortage of labor will remain acute in the coming years.

在未來的幾年中，勞工的短缺仍將是個嚴重問題。

4. Thinking one step ahead will *keep* us competitive.

比他人先未雨綢繆，將有助於我們維持競爭力。

** crash 〔kræʃ〕 *n.* 崩潰　　knell 〔nɛl〕 *n.* 喪鐘

● 演說小教室 ●

"Ask not what your country can do for you, but ask what you can do for your country." 這是美國故總統甘迺迪所說的話，幾乎全美國人都知道。把 your country 改成 your company，就成為老闆或高級主管激勵員工，深具效果的講詞。

像這樣，把大家都知道的**名人格言**稍微變化一下，就可以使演講生動有趣。

Unit 8
The Piracy Problem

• A Sample Speech •

" Taiwan — where the people's smiles are as genuine as your Rolex watch."

It's been a while since we've heard remarks like that. Hong Kong may still be a counterfeiter's paradise, and Bangkok may be the center of every vice known to mankind, but Taiwan has improved. Why? Where have all the copy-watches gone?

The answer is that thousands of them are destroyed every month. That is, the government has been **cracking down on** counterfeit rings of all kinds, from fake perfumes and pirated videcasettes to IBM clones.

Now it takes just as much technical know-how to copy something as to invent it in the first place. As a result of the crackdown, many former counterfeiters are developing their own brands. Soon the process will come to a full circle, and counterfeiters in other countries will be found selling fake Taiwan products.

ADVICE

這篇演說以幽默（humor）的方式開場，帶有自我嘲諷（irony）的意味。在國際社交場合中，針對類似仿冒等問題，難免會碰上指責詢問的尷尬場面，這時適時的自我嘲諷，可以幫助你化危機為轉機。

仿冒問題

● 演說實例 ●

「台灣——人民的微笑和你的勞力士手錶一樣真的地方。」

我們已經有一段時間沒聽見類似的評論了。香港可能還是仿冒者的樂園，而曼谷可能是人類所有罪惡的中心，可是台灣卻已經改善了。為什麼？那些仿製的錶都到哪裏去了？

答案是，每個月都有數以千計的假錶遭到銷毀。也就是說，政府已經開始對各式各樣的仿冒集團，展開嚴厲的取締，包括假香水、盜版錄影帶，及仿造的 IBM 電腦等。

目前，仿冒所需要的技術已經和發明所需要的技術不相上下了。由於政府的掃蕩，許多從前的仿冒商都紛紛發展自己的品牌。很快地，這種程序就會周而復始，人們將會發現其他國家的仿冒者在賣假的台灣產品。

＊＊ genuine〔'dʒɛnjʊɪn〕*adj*. 眞正的　　remark〔rɪ'mɑrk〕*n*. 評論
counterfeiter〔'kaʊntɚˌfɪtɚ〕*n*. 仿冒者
crack down 採取嚴厲的手段　　fake〔fek〕*n*. 僞造品
pirated〔'paɪrətɪd〕*adj*. 盜版的　　clone〔klon〕*n*. 仿製品
brand〔brænd〕*n*. 商標；品牌

Useful Expressions

提出對比

1. Although counterfeiting was once condoned, the government now is cracking down.

   雖然政府曾經不追究仿冒，但是現在政府正展開嚴厲取締。

2. Where manufacturers once copied other brands, now they are selling *under their own brand names*.

   製造商曾經仿冒其他品牌，但現在他們有了屬於自己的品牌。

改善成果

1. We have realized the futility of intellectual piracy.

   我們已了解盜版的無益。

2. We *are* now *engaged in* an information campaign to tell our citizens of the evils of copying other people's products.

   我們正在從事一項資訊活動，告訴我們的人民仿製他人產品的壞處。

3. We do not like to be known as a kingdom of fake products.

   我們不喜歡被認為是仿冒王國。

4. We are *taking steps* to better protect international copyrights and patents.

   我們正逐步著手保護國際間的版權和專利。

5. All in all, over one million bottles of fake perfume were smashed last year.

   總計在去年有超過一百萬瓶的假香水被銷毀。

** condone〔kən'don〕*v.* 原諒；寬恕　futility〔fju'tɪlətɪ〕*n.* 無益
campaign〔kæm'pen〕*n.* 活動　copyright〔'kɑpɪ,raɪt〕*n.* 版權
patent〔'petn̩t, 'pætn̩t〕*n.* 專利　smash〔smæʃ〕*v.* 銷毀

6. ***To begin with***, the police have confiscated thousands of pirated videocasettes.

首先，警方已經沒收了數以千計的盜版錄影帶。

結論

1. We do not like others to copy our products, either.

我們也不喜歡別人仿冒我們的產品。

2. Enforcement is a very difficult task.

強制執行是件困難的工作。

3. In the end, the situation will surely improve.

最後情形一定會改善。

4. All told, Taiwan is changing before our very eyes.

整體來說，台灣正在我們的眼前逐漸改善。

5. The situation has changed for the better.

情況已經好轉了。

** confiscate〔'kɑnfɪs,ket〕*v.* 充公;沒收 videocasette〔'vidɪokæ'sɛt〕*n.* 錄影帶
enforcement〔ɪn'fɔrsmənt,ɛn-,-'fɔrsmənt〕*n.* 強制執行

● 演說小教室 ●

1. Frailty, your name is women. 弱者，你的名字是女人。
   （Shakespeare：莎士比亞，英國詩人，劇作家。1964 — 1616。）

2. Nothing in this world is said to be certain, except death and taxes. 除了死亡和稅，世界上沒有一樣東西是確定的。
   （B. Franklin：富蘭克林，美國政治家，科學家。1706 — 90。）

3. It is better to have loved and lost than never to have loved at all. 愛過然後失去，比從來沒有愛過好。
   （A. Tennyson：但尼生，英國詩人。1809 — 92。）

4. That government is best which governs not at all.
   管得最少的政府就是最好的政府。
   （H.D. Thoreau：梭羅，美國思想家，著作家。1817 — 62。）

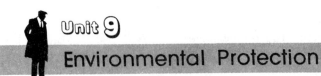

Unit ⑨
Environmental Protection

● A Sample Speech ●

The construction of the new petrochemical plant has been delayed for 2 years now **due to** anti-pollution protests. The people in the locality where we plan to build the plant **have obstructed** our people **from** going into the lot and starting the construction.

If we do not build the plant immediately, shortages of petrochemical raw materials will occur by 1993. **Needless to say**, the delay in the construction of the plant is also being used as an example of the deteriorating investment environment here. That's the reason why the government is on our side.

As far as pollution worries **are concerned**, we can assure the general public that the plant has been fitted with pollution control devices and the standards we have adopted are some of the most stringent in the world. However a lot of people **are** still **haunted by** the bad records of other petrochemical plants in the past. What we need now is to convince them that this is not so anymore. It takes time, but we can and must **make it**.

ADVICE

國內環保意識興起，連帶使得許多居民對化學工業採取否定的態度。面對這個問題，可向外國友人說明，過去不重視環保的慘痛經驗仍然留在人們心中，因此唯有靠業者以環保的誠意與實際行動來化解這種偏見。

環保問題

● 演說實例 ●

　　由於環保意識的升高，已經使新石化工廠的建造拖了二年了。而且當地居民也阻撓我們的人員進入工地興建工程。

　　假如我們不馬上興建這座工廠，在西元一九九三年之前，我們將會有石化原料短缺的危機。不用說，這個興建計畫的延遲也被認為是投資環境愈來愈惡化的例子。這就是為什麼政府要支持我們的理由。

　　就防止環境污染的觀點而言，我們可以向大眾保證，這座工廠已裝了控制污染的設備，而一定能符合世界上最嚴苛的污染防治標準。然而，許多人仍對過去其它石化工廠的不良記錄無法釋懷。我們現在就是要使他們相信，這種情形將不會再出現。這需要花點時間，但我們能夠也必須做好它。

**　construction〔kənˈstrʌkʃən〕*n.* 建築
　petrochemical〔ˌpɛtroˈkɛməkḷ〕*adj.* 石油化學的
　locality〔loˈkælətɪ〕*n.* 位置；所在地
　obstruct〔əbˈstrʌkt〕*v.* 阻隔；遮斷；妨礙
　deteriorate〔dɪˈtɪrɪəˌret〕*v.* 使變壞　　assure〔əˈʃʊr〕*v.* 保證
　stringent〔ˈstrɪndʒənt〕*adj.* 嚴苛的

Useful Expressions

環保意識所引起的負面影響

1. Some people *are against* our plan to build a new chemical plant in their locality due to pollution fears.

由於害怕化學工廠所帶來的污染，有些人士反對我們在當地的興建計畫。

2. Lack of pollution controls in the past still *casts a shadow on* people's faith in chemical factories.

以往缺乏污染防治的情形，依然影響到人們對化學工廠的信心。

3. A lot of people still *hold a negative impression* of all chemical industries, although pollution control devices have made polluting chemical factories a thing of the past.

很多人仍對化學工廠持有負面的印象，雖然污染防治的裝置已使許多污染的化學工廠成為過眼雲煙。

公司的立場

1. We believe that saving the environment is everyone's responsibility.

我們相信環境保護人人有責。

2. Economic growth and environmental concerns should be balanced.

經濟成長與環境保護須齊頭並進。

3. Ensuring the well-being of the environment is a corporate responsibility.

確保更美好的生活環境是企業的責任。

** impression 〔ɪm'prɛʃən〕 *n.* 印象
responsibility 〔rɪ,spɑnsə'bɪlətɪ〕 *n.* 責任
corporate 〔'kɔrpərɪt〕 *adj.* 企業的；團體的

4. We've decided to put our plan into action *in spite of* objections to it.

即使有反對的聲浪，我們仍決定將我們的計畫付諸實行。

結論

1. Some time is needed to change people's attitudes.

改變大衆的態度是需要時間的。

2. We'll do our best to answer their objections by putting in pollution control equipment.

我們會添置完備的污染防治設備以平息民衆的反對聲浪。

3. *We are convinced* that we can balance the money motive and the welfare of the community.

我們有信心能平衡經濟利益與社區團體的福祉。

** objection 〔əbˈdʒɛkʃən〕 *n.* 異議　　attitude 〔ˈætə,tjud〕 *n.* 態度
convince 〔kənˈvɪns〕 *v.* 說服　　motive 〔ˈmotɪv〕 *n.* 目的；動機
welfare 〔ˈwɛl,fɛr〕 *n.* 福利

● 演說小教室 ●

　　根據調查，有**百分之八十**的美國大學生承認，在選修演說課時，仍對講台懷有恐懼感。對國人而言，這個數據可能還更高。恐懼的原因多半是因為**不習慣**，演說對多數人而言是一種**未知**的焦慮,而克服這種羞怯、畏懼的方法之一就是儘量選擇自己**有資格談論**的話題，如以生活經驗，特殊事件等生活瑣事開始説起。讓身邊熟悉的內容，幫助你輕鬆有把握地談下去。

Unit 10
Introducing Taiwan

● A Sample Speech ●

Good afternoon distinguished guests, friends and colleagues. **It's an honor** to be speaking in front of such an accomplished group. I have been asked to speak to you about my country, the Republic of China, otherwise known to you as Taiwan.

Taiwan is known as one of the **four dragon economies of Asia.** It is situated across from Mainland China, bordered by the Philippines to the south, Japan to the north and the vast Pacific Ocean to the east. Taiwan has a sub-tropical climate. As such, It is hot and humid in summer and mildly cold in winter.

Taiwan has undergone many changes through the years. What was once known as a backwater of Asia is now known as a showcase of economic success and prosperity; and this we have achieved in a span of little more than three decades. We are proud of our achievements and by the year 2000 we confidently foresee Taiwan joining the ranks of **developed nations**.

Come visit my country and see for yourself how we've **transformed** this once sleepy island in East Asia **into** one of the most vibrant economies in the world today.

ADVICE

在社交場合中介紹台灣，也算是做好國民外交的第一步。在爲外國友人介紹時，最頭痛的莫過於找不到適合的字彙來表示一些傳統或台灣專有的事物。因此平常就應多注意收集這些詞彙，以備不時之需。

介紹台灣

● 演說實例 ●

　　各位貴賓，朋友及同事們，午安，很榮幸能和這樣一個傑出的團體談談。我要向各位談談我的國家：中華民國，也就是各位所知的台灣。

　　台灣以亞洲四小龍之一而聞名，處於中國大陸對面，南臨菲律賓群島，北臨日本，而東臨太平洋。台灣屬於亞熱帶氣候，夏天濕熱而冬天並不很冷。

　　近年來，台灣已經歷了許多改變，曾經只是亞洲偏僻落後的一個小地方，如今成為經濟成功繁榮的櫥窗，而這些成就是我們在不到三十年的時間中創造出來的。我們以我們的成就為傲，我們更深信在西元 2000 年之前，台灣將列入已開發國家之林。

　　各位應該親自前來參觀，看看我們如何由東亞一個沈睡中的小島，轉變為今日世界上最生氣蓬勃的貿易國家之一。

** distinguished〔dɪ'stɪŋgwɪʃt〕*adj.* 著名的；傑出的
colleague〔'kɑlig〕*n.* 同事　sub-tropical〔sʌb'trɑpɪkḷ〕*adj.* 亞熱帶的
undergo〔ˌʌndɚ'go〕*v.* 經歷；遭遇
backwater〔'bæk,wɔtɚ,-,wɑtɚ〕*n.* 窮鄉僻壤
prosperity〔prɑs'pɛrətɪ〕*n.* 繁榮　foresee〔for'si, fɔr-〕*v.* 預知
transform〔træns'fɔrm〕*v.* 改變　vibrant〔'vaɪbrənt〕*adj.* 充滿生氣的

Useful Expressions

開場白

1. It's a pleasure to introduce my country to you.

很高興爲大家介紹我的國家。

2. I'm here to **share with** you the Cinderella story of Taiwan.

在這兒，我要和大家分享台灣灰姑娘般的故事。

3. I've come here today to talk about my country.

今天我要和各位談談我的國家。

4. Taiwan has generated a lot of curiosity in the international community.

台灣在國際間引起了很多的好奇心。

風土人情

1. Taiwan *is well-know* for its tropical fruit and friendly people.

台灣以熱帶水果和友善的人民聞名。

2. Taiwan is known for its beautiful mountain scenery.

台灣以美麗的山地風光著名。

3. The old culture of China is wonderfully preserved and is fluorishing in Taiwan.

在台灣，中國傳統文化不僅受到妥善保存，而且更加發揚光大。

經濟政治成就

1. We have accomplished something short of an *economic miracle.*

除了經濟奇蹟之外，我們也有其他成就。

** Cinderella〔͵sɪndəˋrɛlə〕*n.* 灰姑娘　preserve〔prɪˋzɝv〕*v.* 保護；保存
flourish〔ˋflɝɪʃ〕*v.* 興盛　　*short of ~* 除去~

2. We have prospered steadily under a democratic system.

在民主制度下，我們很穩定地成長與繁榮。

3. People there are industrious and have been making every effort to build a modern country.

那兒的人都很勤奮，並且一直努力創造一個現代化的國家。

▍結尾

1. Come visit Taiwan.

請來台灣觀光。

2. The Chinese nickname for Taiwan, "*treasure island*" is not without its merit.

台灣別稱寶島並不是憑空得來的。

3. We have a lot to offer you in the paradise called Taiwan.

在台灣這個天堂裏，我們能提供您所需的一切。

** prosper〔'prɑspɚ〕*v.* 興盛；繁榮　　industrious〔ɪn'dʌstrɪəs〕*adj.* 勤奮的
merit〔'mɛrɪt〕*n.* 優點；功績　　paradise〔'pærə,daɪs〕*n.* 天堂；樂園

● 演說小教室 ●

1. Lunar New Year's Day 農曆過年
2. New Year's Eve 除夕　　3. family reunion 團圓飯
4. night market 夜市　　5. Dragon Boat Festival 端午節
6. Mid-autumn Festival 中秋節
7. moon cake 月餅　　8. beef noodles 牛肉麵
9. dragon and lion dance 舞龍舞獅
10. calligraphy〔kə'lɪgrəfɪ〕*n.* 書法
11. Kuomintang 國民黨（ KMT ）
12. Democratic Progressive Party 民進黨（ DPP ）
13. plum rains 梅雨　　14. the plum blossom 梅花
15. Peking opera 平劇

美國的企業組織

在台灣多由**總經理**（ *President* ）握有最高的權力，但在美國則是由**董事長**（ *Chairman* ）擔負最大的責任（ *Chief Executive Officer* ）。另外，美國人「企業是由股東投資而成立」這種意識比國人強烈，因此股東大會常是最高決議機構。

以下是典型的美國企業組織。

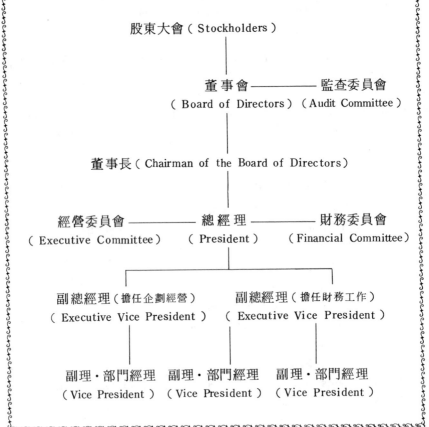

股東大會（ Stockholders ）

董事會―――――監查委員會
（ Board of Directors ）（ Audit Committee ）

董事長（ Chairman of the Board of Directors ）

經營委員會――――總經理―――――財務委員會
（ Executive Committee ）（ President ）（ Financial Committee ）

副總經理（擔任企劃經營）　　副總經理（擔任財務工作）
（ Executive Vice President ）（ Executive Vice President ）

副理・部門經理　副理・部門經理　副理・部門經理
（ Vice President ）（ Vice President ）（ Vice President ）

附錄

會議司儀常用語

● **司儀自我介紹**

♧ My name is Tom Smith and I will **serve as** the chairman of this meeting.

我叫湯姆・史密斯，是這次會議的主席。

● **進行討論**

♧ We shall now **proceed to** the discussion.

現在我們進行討論。

♧ We would like to discuss the plan for introducing our products into the European market.

我們要討論我們產品進軍歐洲市場的計畫。

♧ Let's examine this problem **in further detail**.

讓我們進一步審查這個問題。

♧ If you like, we may continue our discussion on policy.

如果你們願意，我們可以繼續政策的討論。

♧ I would like to discuss the terms of business.

我想討論這筆生意的條件。

♧ Let's discuss the terms and conditions of this commodity transaction.

讓我們討論商品交易的條件。

✱✱ proceed〔prə'sid〕 *v.* 繼續進行
commodity〔kə'mɑdətɪ〕 *n.* 商品

term〔tɜm〕 *n.* 條件

♤ Shall we come to the details of our agreement?   我們將討論合約的細節嗎？

● **徵詢意見**

♤ Please give me your frank opinions.   請坦率地提出意見。

♤ If you have any ideas *on* this matter, please tell me frankly.   如果各位有關於這方面的任何意見，請盡情表達。

♤ We need something effective to solve the problem, so let us have your frank opinion on the matter.   我們需要能有效解決問題的意見，所以請各位坦率地表達對這件事的看法。

● **詢求發言**

♤ Mr. Anderson, would you start?   安德森先生，從您開始好嗎？

♤ Mr. Brown, would you tell me your opinion on this matter?   布朗先生，能告訴我您對這件事的看法嗎？

♤ Mr. Tony Bolder, would you give me your opinion on the work problem?   東尼‧伯德，能不能談談對工作上問題的意見？

♤ Mr. Jackson, what is on your mind?   傑克遜先生，您認為呢？

♤ Would you tell us briefly …?   您可以簡單地告訴我們嗎？

** frank〔fræŋk〕*adj.* 坦白的；率直的
effective〔əˈfɛktɪv, ɪ-〕*adj.* 有效的   briefly〔ˈbriflɪ〕*adv.* 簡單扼要地

♤ Everybody at the meeting is re-quested to **contribute** something **to** help effectively solve the matter. Mr. Wang, what is your idea?

會議中的每一個人都應提供有效解決問題的方法。王先生，你的看法如何？

● **有問題嗎？**

♤ Do you have any questions on your activities here?

您對這裏進行的活動有沒有什麼疑問？

● **徵求建議**

♤ We welcome any suggestions to make our business more suc-cessful.

我們歡迎任何建議，以使我們的業務更加成功。

● **司儀發言**

♤ Please allow me to say a few words on this meeting.

讓我為這次的會議說幾句話。

● **結束會議**

♤ We will close the meeting today. Thank you, all of you.

今天我們將結束會議。謝謝各位。

♤ I would like to express a word of gratitude.

讓我向各位道謝。

＊＊ request〔rɪ'kwɛst〕 v. 要求　　contribute〔kən'trɪbjut〕 v. 貢獻
gratitude〔'grætə,tjud〕 n. 感謝

MEMO

Editorial Staff

- 企劃・編著/ 陳怡平
- 英文撰稿/ Edward C. Yulo
- 校訂/
  劉　毅・王慶銘・林佩汀・陳瑠琍
  劉瑞芬・王蓁蓁・林順隆
- 校閱/
  Nick Veitch・Francesca A. Evans
  Thomas Deneau・Stacy Schultz
  Kirk Kofford・Joanne Beckett
  Jeffrey R. Carr・Chris Virani
  David M. Quesenberry
- 封面設計/ 張鳳儀
- 插畫/ 白雪嬌
- 版面設計/ 張鳳儀
- 版面構成/ 陳燕玉
- 打字/
  黃淑貞・蘇淑玲・倪秀梅・吳秋香

||||||||||||● 學習出版公司門市部 ●||||||||||||||

台北地區：台北市許昌街 10 號 2 樓 TEL：(02)2331-4060・2331-9209
台中地區：台中市綠川東街 32 號 8 樓 23 室
　　　　　TEL：(04)2223-2838

|||||||||||||||||||||||||||||||||||||||||||

商務英語演說

編　　著 / 陳怡平
發　行　所 / 學習出版有限公司　　　☎ (02) 2704-5525
郵 撥 帳 號 / 0512727-2 學習出版社帳戶
登　記　證 / 局版台業 2179 號
印　刷　所 / 裕強彩色印刷有限公司
台 北 門 市 / 台北市許昌街 10 號 2 F　　☎ (02) 2331-4060・2331-9209
台 中 門 市 / 台中市綠川東街 32 號 8 F 23 室　☎ (04) 2223-2838
台灣總經銷 / 紅螞蟻圖書有限公司　　☎ (02) 2795-3656
美國總經銷 / Evergreen Book Store　☎ (818) 2813622
本公司網址　www.learnbook.com.tw
電 子 郵 件　learnbook@learnbook.com.tw

售價：新台幣一百五十元正

2004 年 7 月 1 日一版六刷

ISBN 957-519-275-3